Profiling

The Art of Reading People

Like an Open Book

Daniel Vernan

Table of Contents

Intro

The art and science of profiling have deep roots, stretching back to humanity's earliest efforts to make sense of each other's behaviors, intentions, and identities. Long before it became formalized within modern psychology, the ability to read people was an essential skill for survival, community cohesion, and leadership. By observing appearances, gestures, and speech patterns, our ancestors formed judgments about trustworthiness, threat levels, and character traits. These early practices laid the groundwork for the sophisticated methods we use today.

Ancient Roots of Human Observation

In ancient societies, the ability to interpret others was both a practical necessity and a valuable skill for leaders, healers, and community members. Tribal leaders, for instance, would often make judgments about the intentions of strangers or the sincerity of warriors returning from battle. This rudimentary form of profiling relied heavily on intuitive observation and cultural context. Similarly, shamans and spiritual leaders developed early forms of psychological profiling when attempting to discern hidden motives or diagnose what they perceived as spiritual ailments.

Philosophical writings from the ancient world often touched upon the study of human nature and behavior. In China, Confucius emphasized the understanding of character and ethical behavior, suggesting that outward actions often reveal one's true nature. In ancient Greece, philosophers such as Aristotle and Hippocrates sought to categorize and analyze human behavior, laying the foundations for personality theory and temperaments. Hippocrates' theory of the four humors, which linked bodily fluids to personality types (sanguine, choleric, melancholic, and phlegmatic), was an early attempt to systematize human behavior based on observable traits and internal states.

Profiling in the Medieval and Renaissance Eras

During the medieval period, profiling continued to evolve within the frameworks of religious and legal institutions. The inquisition relied on interrogative techniques to assess guilt, sincerity, and heretical intent. Although often harsh and unethical, these methods marked an early form of behavioral assessment under high-stress circumstances.

The Renaissance era brought new attention to the complexity of human nature. Scholars like Niccolò Machiavelli studied power dynamics and the manipulation of perception to achieve political ends. His works highlighted the role of observation and deceit in human affairs, serving as both a cautionary guide and a framework for understanding social influence.

Art and literature of this period also delved into character studies, revealing an increasing fascination with motivations and inner worlds. The popularity of Shakespearean plays, for instance, underscored the importance of recognizing hidden intentions, subtle behaviors, and psychological conflict.

Scientific Foundations: 18th to 19th Century Developments

The scientific revolution of the 18th and 19th centuries provided a more systematic approach to human behavior. Franz Joseph Gall's development of phrenology—assessing personality traits based on skull shape and structure—captured the interest of many as an early (though later debunked) attempt to link biology to behavior. This period also saw the emergence of criminology, with pioneers like Cesare Lombroso theorizing that certain physical features could indicate criminality. While many of these ideas would later be discredited as pseudoscience, they reflected society's growing interest in objectively understanding human tendencies.

Simultaneously, Sigmund Freud's psychoanalytic theory opened new pathways for exploring the mind's inner workings. Freud's emphasis on unconscious motives and suppressed desires provided deeper insight into why people act as they do, inspiring further exploration of personality, childhood experiences, and human relationships.

Modern Profiling and the Emergence of Psychological Science

By the early 20th century, profiling had begun to take on a more defined structure within psychology and law enforcement. World War II witnessed the advent of criminal profiling as intelligence agencies sought to understand the behavior of enemy leaders. One notable example was the work of American psychiatrist Walter

Langer, who profiled Adolf Hitler based on available intelligence, accurately predicting his behavior as the war drew to a close.

The post-war era brought further refinement to the field. Criminal profilers like Howard Teten and John Douglas at the FBI pioneered modern criminal profiling techniques. They studied crime scene behaviors and developed behavioral analysis tools to identify and track serial offenders. Profiling evolved into a systematic process of inference, merging psychological insights with crime scene evidence to understand and predict offender behavior.

Today, profiling is employed across various disciplines, from criminal justice and corporate hiring to behavioral therapy and negotiation strategy. Modern techniques integrate advances in neuroscience, data analytics, and psychology, creating a nuanced understanding of how internal and external factors shape human behavior.

Chapter One: The Basics of Human Behavior

What Drives Human Behavior

While every individual acts within the bounds of their unique personality and environment, understanding the primary drivers of behavior offers crucial insights into why people do what they do. This knowledge not only sheds light on individual actions but also reveals the forces shaping group dynamics, culture, and societal norms.

Biological Influences: The Roots of Instinct and Physiology

At its core, human behavior is influenced by biological processes rooted in the body's systems. These biological influences can be traced back to our evolutionary history, genetic makeup, brain structure, and hormonal activity.

Evolutionary Instincts and Survival Mechanisms: Human evolution has endowed us with survival-oriented instincts. For example, the "fight, flight, or freeze" response to danger is an automatic reaction designed to protect us from harm. This physiological response, driven by the release of stress hormones like adrenaline and cortisol, prepares the body to respond quickly to threats. Such instincts, though adapted to modern circumstances, often shape everyday behaviors, including how we respond to stress, conflict, and uncertainty.

Genetics and Individual Differences: Genetic inheritance also plays a significant role in shaping personality traits, temperament, and predispositions. Some people are naturally more extroverted or introverted due to inherited tendencies, while others may be predisposed to anxiety or resilience. Behavioral genetics seeks to understand the degree to which genetic factors influence behaviors such as aggression, intelligence, and empathy. While genetic predispositions do not dictate behavior, they create a foundation upon which other influences act.

Brain Function and Neurochemistry: The brain is the command center of human behavior. Different regions of the brain govern emotional responses, decision-making, memory, and social interactions. Neurotransmitters—chemical messengers like dopamine, serotonin, and norepinephrine—play a critical role in regulating mood, motivation, and pleasure. Imbalances in these chemicals can lead to behavioral changes, such as those seen in depression, addiction, and anxiety disorders. Advances in neuroscience have highlighted the powerful impact of brain activity on behavior, showing how complex interactions within the brain shape everyday actions.

Hormonal Influences: Hormones, such as testosterone, estrogen, and oxytocin, influence behavior in profound ways. For example, testosterone is often associated with competitive and aggressive behaviors, while oxytocin, sometimes called the "love hormone," plays a key role in bonding, trust, and social connection. Hormonal fluctuations, whether during puberty, pregnancy, or aging, can impact emotions, motivations, and decision-making processes.

Psychological Influences: The Inner World of Thoughts and Feelings

Psychological factors encompass the cognitive processes, emotions, motivations, and past experiences that drive behavior. These influences reflect the inner workings of the mind and shape how individuals perceive and respond to the world around them.

Cognitive Processes and Perception: Cognition refers to how people process information, form judgments, and make decisions. Perception is central to cognition; it determines how individuals interpret and respond to external stimuli. For instance, two people may perceive the same event differently based on their past experiences, beliefs, and cognitive biases. Cognitive distortions—such as overgeneralization or catastrophic thinking—can lead to maladaptive behaviors, highlighting how thoughts shape actions.

Emotions and Motivation: Emotions are powerful drivers of behavior, often dictating how individuals react to situations and interact with others. Emotions like fear, anger, love, and joy influence choices, relationships, and even physical health. Psychologists have identified various theories of motivation that explain why people act as they do. Abraham Maslow's hierarchy of needs, for example, proposes that people are motivated by a series of needs, beginning with physiological survival and progressing to higher-order desires like self-actualization. The interplay between emotions and motivations often determines goal-setting, ambition, and the ability to persevere in the face of adversity.

Childhood Experiences and Conditioning: Psychological influences are also rooted in past experiences, particularly those from childhood. Early interactions with caregivers shape attachment styles, which in turn influence how individuals form and maintain relationships throughout life. Classical and operant conditioning, as described by pioneers like Ivan Pavlov and B.F. Skinner, reveal how behaviors can be learned or reinforced through reward and punishment. These early experiences contribute to the development of habits, fears, and emotional triggers that persist into adulthood.

Personality Traits and Disorders: Psychologists have identified various personality traits that influence behavior. The Big Five personality traits—openness, conscientiousness, extraversion, agreeableness, and neuroticism—provide a framework for understanding how individuals may react in different situations. For example, highly conscientious people may be more organized and goal-driven, while those high in neuroticism may experience emotional instability. Personality disorders, such as borderline or antisocial personality disorder, further illustrate how deeply ingrained patterns of thinking and behaving can diverge from societal norms.

Social Influences: Culture and Environment

Human beings are inherently social creatures whose behaviors are shaped by interactions with others and the societal norms that guide those interactions. Social influences encompass culture, relationships, social norms, and environmental factors that impact behavior on both an individual and collective level.

Cultural Norms: Culture exerts a significant influence on behavior by establishing norms, values, and traditions. What is considered polite in one culture may be deemed rude in another. Cultural norms shape behaviors ranging from communication styles and body language to gender roles and rituals. Socialization, the process by which individuals learn and internalize cultural values, begins early in life and continues through interactions with family, peers, and institutions.

Social Roles and Expectations: Roles within society, such as those of parent, employee, or friend, come with specific expectations and obligations. These roles shape behavior by providing a script for how one should act in various contexts. Social expectations, whether formal (laws, rules) or informal (social norms, etiquette), guide behavior by establishing boundaries of what is acceptable. Deviating from these norms can lead to social consequences, such as ostracism or disapproval.

Peer Pressure and Group Dynamics: The desire to fit in and belong to a group can have a powerful impact on behavior. Peer pressure often influences adolescents, but it affects people of all ages, shaping behaviors, attitudes, and decisions. Conformity, obedience, and groupthink demonstrate how individuals can be influenced by the opinions and behaviors of those around them. Social psychologists, including Stanley Milgram and Solomon Asch, have explored how authority figures and group dynamics can lead to behaviors that defy individual beliefs or morality.

Environmental Factors: Socioeconomic status, access to resources, and environmental conditions also play a critical role in behavior. Economic hardship, for example, can lead to stress, reduced opportunities, and constrained choices, while wealth may offer freedom but bring its own set of challenges and pressures. Environmental factors, such as living conditions, climate, and community safety, influence health, mental well-being, and behavior. The interplay between these external factors and internal drives often dictates how people navigate their circumstances.

Why We Do What We Do?

Human behavior is often guided by patterns—repeated actions, reactions, or thought processes shaped by a mix of internal drives and external influences. These patterns help us navigate a complex world efficiently, providing structure, predictability, and meaning to our daily lives. However, understanding why we exhibit certain behaviors requires exploring the underlying mechanisms and motivations that drive them.

Habits and Routine Behavior

Habits form the backbone of human behavior. They are actions performed automatically in response to specific triggers or cues, often without conscious thought. From brushing our teeth every morning to checking our phones as soon as we wake up, habits help conserve mental energy by offloading routine tasks to the subconscious mind. Behavioral scientists have long studied the habit loop, which consists of three key elements: cue, routine, and reward. A cue triggers the behavior, the routine is the action itself, and the reward is the benefit gained (such as pleasure, relief, or accomplishment).

Habits can be adaptive or maladaptive, depending on their impact on our well-being. Positive habits, like regular exercise or mindfulness practice, enhance our lives, while negative habits, such as procrastination or excessive screen time, may hinder our goals. The brain's reward system, driven by neurotransmitters like dopamine, plays a crucial role in reinforcing habits. Understanding this loop allows individuals to break unproductive patterns by changing the cues or substituting different rewards.

Defense Mechanisms and Coping Behaviors

When faced with stress, conflict, or anxiety, people often engage in defense mechanisms—psychological strategies that protect their ego and help them cope with emotional pain. These behaviors are often unconscious and can range from healthy coping strategies to more dysfunctional responses. Some common defense mechanisms include:

- **Denial:** Refusing to acknowledge an uncomfortable reality. For example, someone might deny a health problem even when symptoms are apparent.

- **Projection:** Attributing one's own feelings or traits to someone else. This behavior can manifest as accusing others of hostility while feeling hostile oneself.

- **Rationalization:** Creating logical explanations for irrational or unacceptable behavior, often to justify actions or alleviate guilt.

- **Displacement:** Redirecting emotions or impulses from a threatening target to a safer one. For instance, a person frustrated at work might take out their anger on a family member.

While defense mechanisms can offer temporary relief from discomfort, overreliance on them can hinder self-awareness and healthy conflict resolution. More adaptive coping strategies, such as problem-solving, seeking social support, and mindfulness, allow individuals to face stressors constructively.

Social Conformity and Group Behavior

Humans are inherently social creatures, and much of our behavior is shaped by the desire to belong and be accepted by others. Social conformity refers to the tendency to align one's behavior, attitudes, or beliefs with those of a group. This behavior is deeply rooted in the need for social cohesion and can be beneficial, promoting harmony and cooperation within communities.

However, conformity can also lead to negative outcomes, such as peer pressure or groupthink, where critical thinking is overshadowed by the desire for consensus. Studies by social psychologists like Solomon Asch have shown how powerful social influence can be. In Asch's famous conformity experiments, participants were willing to give incorrect answers to simple questions when faced with the unanimous (but incorrect) responses of a group.

Relatedly, **obedience to authority** is another powerful driver of human behavior. Classic studies, such as Stanley Milgram's obedience experiments, reveal how ordinary people can engage in harmful behaviors when instructed by an authority figure. These findings highlight the complex interplay between individual responsibility and social influence.

Cognitive Biases and Heuristics

Behavioral patterns are often influenced by cognitive biases—systematic errors in thinking that affect decision-making and judgments. These biases are the result of mental shortcuts, known as heuristics, that our brains use to process information quickly. While heuristics can be helpful for navigating complex environments, they can also lead to predictable errors and irrational behaviors.

Common cognitive biases include:

- **Confirmation Bias:** The tendency to seek out and favor information that confirms one's existing beliefs while ignoring evidence that contradicts them. This bias can lead to polarized thinking and resistance to change.

- **Availability Heuristic:** Judging the likelihood of an event based on how easily examples come to mind. For instance, people may overestimate the danger of flying after hearing about a plane crash in the news.

- **Anchoring Bias:** Relying too heavily on the first piece of information encountered (the "anchor") when making decisions. Sales tactics often use this bias by setting an initial high price to influence perceptions of value.

- **Sunk Cost Fallacy:** Continuing to invest time, money, or effort into something simply because of previous investments, even when it would be rational to walk away.

Cognitive biases are deeply ingrained in human thought processes, but awareness of these biases can help mitigate their impact and promote more rational decision-making.

Attachment and Relationship Patterns

Attachment theory, developed by psychologist John Bowlby, posits that early experiences with caregivers shape an individual's attachment style, influencing their behavior in relationships throughout life. The four main attachment styles are:

- **Secure Attachment:** Individuals with this style tend to have healthy relationships, trusting others while maintaining a strong sense of self-worth.

- **Anxious Attachment:** People with this style often seek constant reassurance from partners, fearing abandonment and rejection.

- **Avoidant Attachment:** Those with avoidant attachment may struggle with intimacy, distancing themselves emotionally from others.

- **Disorganized Attachment:** This style is characterized by a mix of contradictory behaviors, often rooted in unresolved trauma or inconsistent caregiving.

Attachment patterns influence behaviors such as communication, conflict resolution, and emotional regulation in relationships. Recognizing these patterns can help individuals improve their interactions and cultivate more fulfilling connections.

Motivation and Goal-Directed Behavior

Motivation is a key driver of human behavior, directing actions toward specific goals or outcomes. Psychologists have identified various types of motivation, including intrinsic (driven by internal satisfaction) and extrinsic (driven by external rewards). Theories such as Maslow's hierarchy of needs and Self-Determination Theory (SDT) explore how individuals prioritize and pursue different goals based on their desires for autonomy, competence, and connection.

Understanding one's motivations can clarify why certain behaviors persist and how they align with personal values. It also highlights potential areas for growth, such as shifting from extrinsic rewards (e.g., money or recognition) to intrinsic fulfillment (e.g., purpose and personal growth).

Recognizing and Avoiding Biases in Observing Others

Human beings have an inherent tendency to form judgments and make sense of their world through observation. While our ability to analyze and interpret the actions, words, and behaviors of others is essential for social interaction and decision-making, it is often influenced by biases—systematic errors in thinking that can distort perceptions. Biases can lead to inaccurate conclusions, unfair judgments, and flawed decisions, both in personal interactions and in broader societal contexts.

The Nature of Cognitive Biases: Why They Exist

Cognitive biases are mental shortcuts that allow the brain to process information quickly. While these shortcuts can be efficient and useful for navigating complex social environments, they can also lead to flawed observations. The human mind evolved to prioritize speed over accuracy in some situations—such as recognizing potential threats—but in modern contexts, these biases can result in unfair or inaccurate judgments.

Biases often emerge from our need to simplify complex realities, reinforce existing beliefs, and protect our sense of self. They are shaped by personal experiences, cultural conditioning, social influences, and cognitive patterns. While everyone is susceptible to biases, becoming aware of their presence is the first step in minimizing their impact on our observations and judgments.

Common Biases in Observing Others

To effectively recognize and avoid biases, it is important to understand some of the most common ones that influence how we perceive and evaluate others:

Confirmation Bias: Confirmation bias is the tendency to seek out, interpret, and remember information that confirms our preexisting beliefs while ignoring or dismissing evidence that contradicts them. When observing others, confirmation bias can lead us to selectively notice behaviors that align with our assumptions, while disregarding behaviors that challenge those assumptions. For example, if we believe that a colleague is uncooperative, we may focus on instances where they refuse to collaborate and overlook times when they are helpful.

Fundamental Attribution Error: The fundamental attribution error occurs when we attribute someone's behavior to their personality or character while underestimating the influence of situational factors. If a person arrives late to a meeting, we might assume they are irresponsible or disorganized, without considering external factors like traffic or an emergency. This bias often leads to unfair judgments about others while excusing our own behavior based on context (a phenomenon known as the actor-observer bias).

Stereotyping and Implicit Bias: Stereotyping involves generalizing characteristics about a group of people and applying those assumptions to individuals within the group. Implicit biases are unconscious attitudes or stereotypes that influence how we perceive and treat others. These biases can affect our observations and decisions, even if we consciously reject prejudiced beliefs. For example, research has shown that implicit biases can impact hiring decisions, interactions with law enforcement, and healthcare outcomes.

Halo and Horn Effect: The halo effect occurs when we form a positive impression of someone based on a single favorable characteristic, which then colors our perception of their other traits. Conversely, the horn effect occurs when one negative trait leads to an overall negative impression. For example, if someone is perceived as charismatic, we might overlook their shortcomings or unethical behavior (halo effect). Alternatively, if someone makes a poor first impression, we might dismiss their subsequent positive contributions (horn effect).

Anchoring Bias: Anchoring bias occurs when we rely too heavily on the first piece of information we receive about a person or situation. This initial "anchor" influences how we interpret new information, even if it is unrelated or irrelevant. For example, if a job candidate is introduced as "highly recommended," our perception of their performance during an interview may be skewed by this positive anchor.

Recognizing and Reducing

While biases are a natural part of human cognition, there are strategies that can help us recognize and mitigate their impact on our observations and judgments:

Develop Self-Awareness: Recognizing biases begins with self-awareness. Take time to reflect on your beliefs, assumptions, and automatic reactions when observing others. Question why you perceive someone in a particular way and whether any preconceived notions might be influencing your interpretation. Self-reflection and mindfulness practices can help you become more aware of your biases as they arise.

Seek Diverse Perspectives: Engaging with people who hold different perspectives and backgrounds can challenge your assumptions and broaden your understanding.

Exposure to diversity helps reduce stereotyping and encourages open-mindedness. When observing others, actively seek out alternative explanations and interpretations that differ from your initial judgments.

Focus on Context: Consider the situational factors that may be influencing someone's behavior. Ask yourself whether external circumstances, such as stress, cultural norms, or environmental conditions, might explain their actions. This approach reduces the tendency to make purely personality-based judgments and fosters a more empathetic perspective.

Use Structured Observation Methods: In professional contexts, such as hiring or performance evaluations, using structured observation and assessment methods can help minimize bias. For example, developing clear criteria for evaluating candidates or behaviors and using standardized questions can reduce the influence of subjective impressions and ensure a more objective evaluation process.

Challenge Stereotypes and Assumptions: When you notice yourself making assumptions based on stereotypes or generalized beliefs, take a moment to challenge their validity. Consider whether you have sufficient evidence to support your observations or if you are relying on biases. Remind yourself that individuals are complex and cannot be fully defined by a single trait or group identity.

Practice Empathy and Curiosity: Approach observations with empathy and a genuine desire to understand others. Ask open-ended questions to learn more about a person's motivations, experiences, and perspectives. Curiosity allows you to move beyond superficial judgments and fosters deeper connections and mutual respect.

Regularly Reflect on Your Observations: Take time to review your observations and decisions, especially when they involve important judgments about others. Consider whether biases may have influenced your conclusions and, if so, how you can adjust your perspective. This practice helps develop a habit of critical self-reflection and continuous improvement.

Chapter Two: Profiling Through Body Language

Decoding Basic Non-Verbal Cues

Human communication extends far beyond words. In fact, a significant portion of communication is non-verbal, conveyed through body language, gestures, facial expressions, and posture. These non-verbal cues often reveal what people are truly thinking or feeling, even when their words suggest otherwise. By decoding posture, gestures, and facial expressions, individuals gain a powerful tool for reading and understanding others.

The Language of Posture: What Body Position Reveals

Posture is a fundamental element of body language that conveys a person's attitude, confidence, and emotional state. How someone stands, sits, or moves can speak volumes, often before they say a word.

Open vs. Closed Posture: Open posture generally involves uncrossed arms and legs, an upright stance, and an exposed chest. This posture suggests confidence, openness, and a willingness to engage. People with open postures are often perceived as approachable, relaxed, and trustworthy. In contrast, closed posture—such as crossed arms, legs pulled close to the body, or hunched shoulders—can indicate defensiveness, discomfort, or resistance. While closed posture may reflect insecurity or stress, it can also simply signify that someone is cold or physically uncomfortable, emphasizing the importance of context in interpretation.

Dominance and Submission in Posture: Posture can also communicate dominance or submission within social interactions. Dominant individuals often stand or sit with expansive gestures, taking up more space (sometimes referred to as "power poses"). They may place their hands on their hips, lean back with their arms stretched, or maintain an upright and wide stance. Conversely, submissive posture is marked by making oneself smaller, such as crossing the arms tightly, slumping the shoulders, or avoiding eye contact. Understanding the dynamics of dominance and submission can help decode power structures and social hierarchies within groups.

Postural Echo and Mirroring: When people feel comfortable and connected, they often unconsciously mirror each other's postures and movements. This phenomenon, known as postural echo, indicates rapport and mutual understanding. Observing whether someone mirrors your movements can provide clues about their level of comfort and engagement during an interaction.

Gestures: The Movements that Speak

Gestures are movements of the hands, arms, or other body parts that communicate meaning, often accompanying speech to emphasize or clarify a point. Some gestures are universal, while others are culturally specific.

Illustrative Gestures: Illustrative gestures accompany spoken words and serve to clarify or emphasize what is being said. For example, pointing to an object, making hand movements to describe the shape of something, or using a chopping motion to underline a key point are all illustrative gestures. People who use frequent and animated gestures often come across as more engaged and passionate, while limited use of gestures can suggest formality or detachment.

Emblems and Culturally Defined Gestures: Emblems are gestures with specific meanings within a particular culture, such as a thumbs-up (signifying approval or agreement in many Western cultures) or the "OK" hand sign. It is essential to consider cultural context, as gestures that are positive in one culture may be offensive in another. For example, a nod for "yes" and a shake for "no" are common in many cultures, but there are exceptions where these meanings are reversed.

Signs of Stress or Discomfort: Adaptors are gestures that often indicate nervousness, stress, or discomfort. These include behaviors like tapping the feet, biting nails, fidgeting with clothing, or playing with hair. While adaptors can signal anxiety, they can also be habitual and context-dependent. For example, someone tapping their fingers during a long meeting may simply be bored rather than stressed. Paying attention to clusters of behaviors rather than isolated gestures is crucial for accurate interpretation.

Regulators: Regulators are gestures that help control the flow of conversation. Nodding, for example, signals agreement or encourages the speaker to continue. Raising a hand or making a "stop" motion can indicate a desire to interrupt or pause the conversation. Observing regulators helps in understanding social dynamics and conversational intentions.

The Face: The Window to Emotion

Facial expressions are among the most powerful and universal non-verbal cues for conveying emotions. While some expressions are culturally influenced, many are recognized across the world. Psychologist Paul Ekman identified six basic emotions that are universally expressed and recognized: happiness, sadness, fear, anger, surprise, and disgust. These core expressions provide a foundation for interpreting more nuanced emotional cues.

Eye Contact and Eye Behavior: The eyes are often described as the "windows to the soul" because of their role in expressing emotion and intent. Sustained eye contact can indicate interest, confidence, or attraction, while avoiding eye contact may signal discomfort, guilt, or shyness. However, cultural norms play a role; in some cultures, avoiding eye contact is a sign of respect. Eye movements, such as blinking rate, pupil dilation, and gaze direction, also provide important cues. For example, dilated pupils may indicate attraction or heightened interest, while frequent blinking can be a sign of stress or deception.

Mouth and Lips: The mouth is another key area for decoding facial expressions. A genuine smile, known as the Duchenne smile, involves both the mouth and the muscles around the eyes. Fake smiles, by contrast, often engage only the mouth, with no eye involvement. Lip movements can also indicate tension or hesitation, such as pursed lips (suggesting disapproval or stress) or lip biting (potentially signaling anxiety or contemplation). Small changes in mouth movements, such as smirking, clenching, or pouting, can reveal a range of emotions, from amusement to frustration.

Expressions of Emotion in Context: Facial expressions are often most accurately interpreted when considered within the context of the overall situation and accompanying verbal and non-verbal cues. For example, a raised eyebrow might signal curiosity, surprise, or skepticism, depending on the context. Accurate decoding requires paying attention to clusters of cues and considering the broader context of the interaction.

Micro-Expressions and What They Reveal About True Emotions

Micro-expressions are rapid, involuntary facial expressions that reveal true emotions, often occurring within a fraction of a second. Unlike more prolonged or deliberate facial expressions, micro-expressions are difficult to control or suppress, making them an invaluable tool for understanding a person's genuine feelings and intentions. While most people may not consciously detect these fleeting expressions, those trained in observing them can gain deep insights into what someone is truly experiencing beneath the surface of their words or outward demeanor.

Micro-expressions occur because of the way the brain processes emotions, particularly under conditions of high stakes, stress, or when a person is attempting to conceal their true feelings. Emotions are controlled by the limbic system, an older part of the brain responsible for automatic responses to emotional stimuli. When we experience a strong emotion—such as fear, anger, joy, or disgust—the limbic system responds immediately, often before conscious control kicks in. As a result, the true emotion is briefly displayed on the face, even if the individual tries to mask it with a neutral or different expression.

Psychologist Paul Ekman, a pioneer in the study of facial expressions, found that micro-expressions are universal across cultures. This means that people from diverse backgrounds can exhibit the same brief facial cues in response to specific emotions. This universality highlights the biological basis of micro-expressions, making them a powerful tool for cross-cultural communication and understanding.

Key Micro-Expressions and Their Meanings

Micro-expressions correspond to the six basic emotions identified by Ekman: happiness, sadness, fear, anger, surprise, and disgust. Each of these emotions has distinct facial cues that can be observed, even if they appear for only a split second.

Happiness

A micro-expression of genuine happiness involves the movement of two key areas: the corners of the mouth lift upward, creating a smile, and the muscles around the eyes (known as the orbicularis oculi) contract, causing "crow's feet" wrinkles and a slight narrowing of the eyes. A genuine smile is known as a Duchenne smile, while a fake or social smile typically involves only the mouth.

Sadness

Sadness is often indicated by drooping eyelids, a downward pull at the corners of the mouth, and a slight lowering of the brow. The inner corners of the eyebrows may also raise, creating a distinctive expression. This expression, even when brief, suggests deep emotional pain or sorrow that someone may be trying to hide.

Fear

The micro-expression of fear is characterized by wide eyes, with the upper eyelids lifted and the lower lids tense. The mouth may be slightly open, as if gasping, and the eyebrows are raised and drawn together. This expression reflects a perception of threat or danger, whether real or anticipated.

Anger

Anger manifests as a lowering and drawing together of the eyebrows, a tightening of the lips, and flaring of the nostrils. The eyes may appear intense or piercing. While overt anger may be easy to spot, a brief flash of this expression—such as in response to a challenging question—can reveal hidden irritation or hostility.

Surprise

Surprise is marked by raised eyebrows, wide-open eyes, and an open mouth. The expression is usually short-lived, as surprise quickly shifts to another emotion, such as joy or fear. The brevity and intensity of this micro-expression provide clues about how unexpected or significant the stimulus is.

Disgust

The micro-expression of disgust involves a wrinkling of the nose, raised upper lip, and sometimes a slight narrowing of the eyes. This expression indicates strong aversion or rejection. Disgust can be directed toward physical stimuli, like unpleasant smells, or toward social situations and behaviors.

How to Observe and Interpret Micro-Expressions

Observing micro-expressions requires focus, patience, and practice. Because these expressions can last as little as 1/25th of a second, they often go unnoticed without conscious attention. Training programs and practice exercises, such as those developed by Ekman, help individuals learn to spot and interpret these fleeting cues accurately.

Pay Attention to Changes in Expression: When observing someone, it is important to notice any sudden changes in their facial expressions, even if they are momentary. Micro-expressions often flash before a person adopts a more deliberate or socially appropriate expression. By paying attention to these fleeting cues, you can better understand their true feelings.

Consider Context and Baseline Behavior: Accurate interpretation of micro-expressions depends on context. While a micro-expression can reveal what someone is feeling, it does not necessarily explain why. It is essential to consider the surrounding environment, the nature of the conversation, and the person's baseline behavior (i.e., their typical mannerisms and reactions) before drawing conclusions. For example, a brief expression of fear during a routine meeting may indicate discomfort with the topic being discussed, while fear in a dangerous situation has more obvious implications.

Look for Clusters of Cues: Micro-expressions are most informative when observed alongside other non-verbal cues, such as body posture, gestures, and tone of voice. Clusters of cues reinforce the interpretation of emotions. For example, a person displaying a micro-expression of anger may also cross their arms tightly, clench their fists, or adopt a rigid posture. This combination of signals provides a more complete picture of their emotional state.

Reading Incongruence Between Words and Actions

One of the most telling indicators of a person's true thoughts, emotions, or intentions is the alignment—or lack thereof—between their words and their actions. When verbal communication does not match non-verbal cues or behaviors, it creates a sense of incongruence that can reveal hidden feelings, internal conflicts, or even attempts to deceive. Learning to recognize and interpret these inconsistencies is a valuable skill that can enhance personal relationships, improve professional interactions, and protect against manipulation or dishonesty.

Incongruence occurs when there is a discrepancy between what a person says and what they do or how they express themselves non-verbally. For example, someone who insists that they are calm while visibly trembling, fidgeting, or clenching their fists is demonstrating incongruence. This mismatch suggests that the person's verbal message does not fully reflect their internal state or true feelings.

Incongruence can manifest in various ways:

- **Non-verbal cues that contradict words:** For example, saying "I'm fine" with a flat or strained voice, avoiding eye contact, or displaying a tense posture.

- **Behavioral actions that contradict spoken commitments:** For instance, someone who promises to be supportive but fails to show up when needed.

- **Tone and delivery that contradict content:** A person may express an apology with insincerity, indicated by a lack of eye contact, a sarcastic tone, or dismissive gestures.

Common Causes of Incongruence

Understanding why incongruence arises is essential for accurately interpreting its meaning. There are several reasons why people may exhibit incongruence between their words and actions:

Emotional Conflict or Ambivalence: People often experience mixed feelings or internal conflicts about a particular issue, leading to incongruent behavior. For example, someone who verbally expresses enthusiasm about a new job opportunity may simultaneously display signs of hesitation, such as shifting eyes or a forced smile.

This incongruence could indicate underlying fear, self-doubt, or a reluctance to leave their current position.

Social Pressure and Expectations: Incongruence may arise when individuals feel compelled to conform to social norms or expectations that conflict with their true feelings. For instance, someone may agree to participate in an activity to avoid disappointing others, even though their body language shows discomfort or reluctance. In such cases, the desire to be accepted or avoid conflict creates a gap between verbal agreement and genuine intent.

Deception and Dishonesty: In some cases, incongruence is a sign of deliberate deception. When people lie, they often struggle to maintain consistency between their words and non-verbal cues because deception requires significant cognitive effort. A person telling a lie might exhibit micro-expressions of fear or guilt, avoid eye contact, or use overly elaborate gestures to reinforce their story. While incongruence alone does not prove dishonesty, it can be a red flag that warrants further scrutiny.

Stress and Anxiety: High levels of stress or anxiety can lead to incongruent behavior, even in people who are not intentionally trying to mislead. Nervousness may cause someone to stammer, fidget, or offer evasive answers, creating the impression of insincerity or confusion. Understanding that stress can contribute to incongruence helps distinguish between genuine anxiety and intentional deceit.

Lack of Self-Awareness: Sometimes, people may be unaware of their true feelings or motivations. A lack of self-awareness can result in incongruent communication, where someone's words contradict their underlying emotions. For example, a person who claims they are not angry but exhibits clenched fists and a tense jaw may not have fully processed their own emotions.

How to Recognize Incongruence Between Words and Actions

Accurately identifying incongruence requires careful observation of both verbal and non-verbal cues. Here are some key areas to focus on:

Body Language and Posture: Pay attention to a person's posture, gestures, and movements. Signs of incongruence include crossed arms (suggesting defensiveness) while verbally expressing agreement, fidgeting during serious statements, or adopting a closed posture while claiming to be open to discussion.

Facial Expressions: Facial expressions often betray true emotions, even when words do not. Micro-expressions—brief flashes of genuine emotion—may appear before a person masks their feelings with a different expression. For example, a fleeting look of contempt may surface before someone offers a polite compliment, signaling potential insincerity.

Tone of Voice and Speech Patterns: The way a person speaks can reveal hidden emotions or intentions. A monotone or hesitant tone may contradict enthusiastic words, while an overly forceful delivery might indicate overcompensation or discomfort. Hesitations, changes in speech pace, or stammering can also suggest internal conflict or stress.

Consistency Over Time: Incongruence often becomes evident when words and actions are inconsistent over time. For instance, a manager who repeatedly promises to support their team but fails to follow through on those promises is demonstrating behavioral incongruence. Patterns of inconsistency are often more telling than isolated instances.

Responding to Incongruence

When you detect incongruence in someone's words and actions, it is important to approach the situation thoughtfully and respectfully. Here are some strategies for addressing it:

Ask Clarifying Questions: Instead of jumping to conclusions, seek clarification by asking open-ended questions. For example, if someone says they are happy but appears withdrawn, you might ask, "How are you really feeling about this?" This invites the person to reflect and potentially reveal underlying emotions.

Offer Empathy and Support: Recognize that incongruence may stem from internal struggles or social pressures. Responding with empathy, rather than judgment, encourages open communication. Expressing understanding and support can help the person feel more comfortable sharing their true feelings.

Pay Attention to Context: Consider the context in which incongruence arises. Stressful situations, social dynamics, or personal history may all influence behavior. Understanding the surrounding factors helps interpret incongruence more accurately and prevents hasty judgments.

Trust Your Instincts, But Verify: When incongruence suggests potential deception or hidden motives, it is important to remain observant without jumping to conclusions. Seek additional information or corroboration to understand the situation fully. Trusting your instincts can be valuable, but relying solely on incongruence as evidence can lead to misunderstandings.

Chapter Three: Speech Patterns and Conversation Analysis

Language is one of humanity's most powerful tools, shaping our thoughts, emotions, relationships, and even our perception of reality. While words convey explicit meaning, they also carry implicit messages that can reveal deeper truths about a person's feelings, intentions, and attitudes. Word choice, phrasing, and tone work together to create layers of meaning that go beyond what is said on the surface. By carefully analyzing how people use language, we can gain insight into their state of mind, their relationship dynamics, and their underlying motivations.

Word Choice

The words people choose to use—consciously or unconsciously—often reflect their inner thoughts and emotional state. Even when discussing mundane topics, word choice can reveal biases, fears, values, or hidden agendas.

Connotation and Implicit Meaning: Many words carry connotations that go beyond their dictionary definitions. For example, referring to someone as "determined" versus "stubborn" conveys very different judgments about the same behavior. While "determined" implies positive perseverance, "stubborn" suggests negative inflexibility. By paying attention to word connotations, we can gain a deeper understanding of how someone feels about a person, event, or situation.

Inclusive vs. Exclusive Language: The use of inclusive or exclusive language can indicate a person's approach to collaboration and relationships. Phrases such as "we should" or "let's try" suggest teamwork and a sense of unity, whereas language like "I think you should" or "it's your responsibility" may signal distance, authority, or blame-shifting. Inclusive language fosters connection and shared ownership, while exclusive language may create division or hierarchy.

Use of Qualifiers and Intensifiers: Qualifiers and intensifiers modify the strength of statements, often reflecting uncertainty, emphasis, or exaggeration. Phrases like "I think," "maybe," or "kind of" can indicate hesitation or a lack of confidence. On the other hand, intensifiers such as "absolutely," "completely," or "never" may convey strong conviction or hyperbole. Careful analysis of these linguistic choices can help discern whether someone is being assertive, tentative, or emotionally charged.

Metaphors and Analogies: People often use metaphors and analogies to make sense of complex experiences or emotions. By examining these linguistic choices, we can gain insight into how they perceive a situation. For example, someone describing a challenging project as "an uphill battle" is framing it as a struggle, while another person referring to the same project as "a puzzle" may view it as a stimulating challenge. Understanding the metaphors people use can reveal their mindset and approach to problem-solving.

Tone of Voice: The Unspoken Message

While words convey meaning, the tone of voice adds context, emotion, and intent. Tone can dramatically alter the meaning of a statement, transforming neutral words into expressions of anger, sarcasm, joy, or fear. Tone encompasses pitch, volume, pacing, and intonation, all of which work together to convey the speaker's emotional state.

Pitch and Volume: Changes in pitch and volume can signal shifts in emotion. A raised voice may indicate excitement, anger, or urgency, while a lower, quieter tone might suggest sadness, fatigue, or secrecy. Similarly, a monotonous tone can convey disinterest or detachment. Paying attention to fluctuations in pitch and volume helps listeners identify the emotional undercurrents of a conversation.

Pacing and Pauses: The pace at which someone speaks can reflect their state of mind. Rapid speech may signal anxiety, excitement, or a desire to persuade, while slow speech can suggest careful thought, hesitation, or a relaxed state. Pauses—whether brief or extended—are equally telling. Strategic pauses can emphasize key points, while unintentional hesitations may reveal uncertainty, stress, or a struggle to articulate complex emotions.

Intonation and Emphasis: Intonation refers to the rise and fall of pitch in spoken language, which adds nuance to words. Placing emphasis on different parts of a sentence can change its meaning entirely. For example, consider the sentence, "I didn't say you stole the book." Emphasizing different words alters the implication:

- "**I** didn't say you stole the book" suggests someone else might have said it.

- "I didn't **say** you stole the book" implies that the speaker communicated it non-verbally or in another manner.

- "I didn't say **you** stole the book" shifts the focus to someone else potentially being the thief.

Analyzing intonation and emphasis helps uncover the subtleties of meaning and intention behind spoken words.

Emotional Cues and Linguistic Patterns

Language is deeply intertwined with emotion. Emotional cues embedded in word choice and tone offer insight into a speaker's feelings, motivations, and interpersonal dynamics.

Expressing Uncertainty or Doubt: People often use hedging language, such as "I guess," "it seems like," or "probably," to soften their statements or express uncertainty. This language pattern can indicate a lack of confidence, fear of judgment, or genuine ambiguity. By recognizing such cues, listeners can probe further to clarify the speaker's intentions or provide reassurance.

Hostility or Aggression in Language: Aggressive language patterns, such as name-calling, condescending remarks, or sarcasm, often signal underlying frustration, anger, or conflict. Even subtle shifts in tone—such as an exaggerated "really?" or dismissive laughter—can convey disdain or disrespect. Identifying these cues allows for a more accurate assessment of the speaker's emotions and provides an opportunity to address tension constructively.

Positive and Negative Framing: The way people frame their words reflects their perspective and attitude toward a topic. Positive framing (e.g., "We have an opportunity to improve") conveys optimism and motivation, while negative framing (e.g., "This situation is a mess") suggests pessimism or resignation. By analyzing the framing of language, we can understand the speaker's outlook and potentially reframe conversations for more productive outcomes.

The Impact of Context on Language Interpretation

Word choice and tone cannot be fully understood without considering context. The meaning of a phrase can change based on the speaker's relationship with the listener, the setting, cultural norms, and the broader situation. Misinterpreting context can lead to misunderstandings or unintended conflict.

Cultural and Social Influences: Different cultures have distinct norms for communication. In some cultures, indirect language and subtle hints are preferred, while in others, direct and assertive communication is valued. Similarly, tone and word choice may reflect respect, formality, or intimacy depending on social roles and hierarchies. Recognizing these contextual factors ensures more accurate interpretation of language.

Emotional State and Environment: The speaker's emotional state and the environment in which communication occurs also influence word choice and tone. Stressful situations may lead to abrupt language, while relaxed settings may encourage warmth and humor. Understanding these factors helps separate transient emotions from deeper intentions or personality traits.

Detecting Lies, Evasions, and Omissions in Communication

Detecting lies, evasions, and omissions in communication is a complex skill that requires careful observation of verbal and non-verbal cues. People lie or withhold information for various reasons, such as self-protection, avoiding conflict, gaining an advantage, or sparing someone else's feelings. While no single behavior can definitively prove deception, certain patterns and inconsistencies can offer strong clues. By combining knowledge of language, body language, and contextual factors, we can better identify when someone may be hiding the truth.

Verbal Indicators of Deception

Deceptive communication often manifests through specific verbal cues that indicate discomfort, inconsistency, or evasion. While these signals should be interpreted with caution and considered within context, they can be valuable tools for detecting dishonesty.

Inconsistent or Contradictory Statements: One of the most telling signs of deception is inconsistency in a person's story. When someone is lying, they may struggle to keep track of their fabricated details, leading to contradictions over time. Asking clarifying questions or revisiting details can help reveal these inconsistencies. If a person's narrative changes or key details shift without explanation, it may indicate that they are not being truthful.

Overly Complex or Vague Responses: Liars often provide excessive detail in an attempt to appear credible or distract from the core issue. This "too much information" strategy may involve unnecessary descriptions or tangential points that are unrelated to the question at hand. Conversely, some people resort to vague or evasive responses, giving little concrete information or speaking in generalities. Phrases like "I don't remember" or "it was just some stuff" can be a sign of reluctance to disclose specific facts.

Qualifying Language and Distancing Statements: People who lie often use qualifying language or distance themselves from their statements. Qualifiers such as "to be honest," "to the best of my knowledge," or "if I recall correctly" may indicate a lack of confidence in what they are saying. Distancing language involves the use of impersonal terms or the avoidance of first-person pronouns. For example, saying "the money went missing" instead of "I lost the money" creates psychological distance from the event.

Lack of Directness and Avoidance of Questions: Evasive communication is characterized by indirect answers, deflection, or refusal to respond to specific questions. If someone frequently changes the subject, answers a question with another question, or provides unrelated responses, it may signal an attempt to avoid the truth. Persistent avoidance of direct answers, especially when coupled with visible discomfort, is a potential indicator of deception.

Speech Patterns and Hesitation: Changes in speech patterns, such as sudden pauses, stammering, or fluctuations in speech rate, may indicate stress or discomfort associated with lying. While hesitation can result from nervousness, it may also reflect the cognitive effort required to fabricate or conceal information. In some cases, people who lie speak too quickly or rush through their explanations, possibly to minimize scrutiny.

Non-Verbal Cues of Dishonesty

Body language and facial expressions often reveal more than words. While people may attempt to control their speech to deceive others, non-verbal cues are more difficult to manipulate and can inadvertently expose their true feelings.

Micro-Expressions and Facial Cues: Micro-expressions are brief, involuntary facial movements that reveal genuine emotions. For example, a person who claims to be happy but briefly displays a flash of fear or disgust may be hiding their true feelings. Detecting these fleeting expressions requires keen observation and practice but can provide powerful clues about hidden emotions.

Eye Behavior and Gaze Patterns: Eye behavior is often associated with lying, but it should be interpreted carefully to avoid overgeneralization. Contrary to popular belief, liars do not always avoid eye contact; some may maintain intense eye contact to appear credible. Rapid blinking, pupil dilation, or shifting gaze may indicate discomfort, but they can also be signs of stress unrelated to lying. Sudden changes in eye behavior during a conversation, such as darting eyes or prolonged glances at exit points, may signal anxiety or a desire to end the interaction.

Body Posture and Gestures: Body language cues such as crossing arms, shifting weight, or turning away from the listener can indicate defensiveness or discomfort. Fidgeting, touching the face, covering the mouth, or scratching the neck may suggest nervousness or self-soothing behavior, both of which are common when someone feels caught or under scrutiny. Incongruent gestures—where non-verbal actions do not match spoken words—also suggest deception. For example, nodding while denying something may reveal internal conflict.

Minimal or Overemphasized Gestures: Liars may either restrict their gestures to avoid "leaking" their true feelings or use exaggerated movements to appear more convincing. Restricted gestures, such as keeping hands rigidly at the sides or making few movements, suggest a conscious effort to control body language. Conversely, overemphasized hand movements or theatrical gestures can indicate an attempt to reinforce a lie.

Detecting Evasions and Omissions

Omissions—leaving out important details—are a common form of deception, as they involve withholding rather than fabricating information. Detecting omissions requires paying attention to what is not said and noticing gaps in the narrative.

Gaps in the Story: When someone omits information, their story may lack key details or logical connections. If a narrative feels incomplete or contains unexplained gaps, it may indicate that the person is leaving out important facts. Asking follow-up questions that probe these gaps can reveal whether the omission is intentional.

Changes in Detail and Level of Specificity: A person who omits details may use vague language, gloss over important moments, or avoid providing specifics. In contrast, when pressed for details, liars may suddenly change their level of specificity or provide inconsistent information. For example, someone who initially claims, "I was out running errands" may later add inconsistent details when questioned further, signaling an attempt to obscure the truth.

Redirecting and Deflecting: Evasions often involve redirecting attention away from the topic in question. This can take the form of changing the subject, minimizing the significance of an issue, or shifting blame onto others. While redirection may sometimes be benign, persistent deflection is often a red flag for dishonesty.

The Contextual Nature of Detecting Deception

It is important to remember that no single behavior, word, or gesture definitively proves deception. People exhibit nervousness, hesitation, and discomfort for many reasons, and cultural differences, social norms, and individual traits can all influence communication styles. Effective detection requires analyzing patterns of behavior, considering context, and weighing verbal and non-verbal cues together.

Baseline Behavior: Establishing a baseline for a person's typical behavior is essential for accurately detecting deception. Everyone has unique communication habits; what appears suspicious for one person may be normal for another. By observing how someone behaves under relaxed, truthful circumstances, you can better detect deviations from their baseline when they may be withholding the truth or lying.

Patterns of Speech Under Stress or Pressure

When individuals experience stress or pressure, their communication often undergoes noticeable changes. These shifts in speech patterns reflect the body and mind's response to heightened emotional states, including anxiety, fear, frustration, or urgency. By learning to identify these changes, we can improve empathy, communication, and even identify underlying issues that may need addressing.

Speech Rate and Pacing

One of the most immediate indicators of stress is a change in the rate of speech. People under pressure may either speed up their speech or slow it down, depending on their personality, the source of the stress, and their coping style.

Rapid Speech In high-stress situations, some individuals speak quickly as their mind races to process information or find a way to respond. Rapid speech often reflects heightened arousal, anxiety, or fear and may be accompanied by other signs of stress, such as shallow breathing or a tense posture. This accelerated pace can make it difficult for the speaker to articulate their thoughts clearly, leading to jumbled words, incomplete sentences, or filler words like "uh," "um," or "you know."

Slowed Speech: Conversely, stress can also cause people to slow down their speech as they become more deliberate and cautious with their words. This pacing often results from a desire to avoid making mistakes, saying the wrong thing, or revealing too much information. Slowed speech may also indicate cognitive overload or emotional overwhelm, where the speaker struggles to find the right words due to mental fatigue or emotional strain.

Hesitations and Pauses

Frequent hesitations and long pauses are common when someone is under stress. These breaks in speech often reflect the person's internal effort to process complex emotions, weigh their words carefully, or manage conflicting thoughts. Stress-induced pauses can also be a sign of self-censorship, where the speaker is wary of saying something they may later regret or that could have negative consequences.

Filler Words and Verbal Tics: Under pressure, people may rely more heavily on filler words like "uh," "um," "like," and "you know" as they search for the right words or stall for time. These verbal tics can serve as a buffer, giving the speaker a moment to think. While occasional use of fillers is normal in conversation, excessive reliance on them may indicate nervousness or difficulty articulating thoughts clearly.

Broken Sentences and Self-Corrections: Stress can lead to frequent self-corrections, where the speaker interrupts themselves to rephrase or clarify what they are trying to say. This pattern reflects a heightened state of self-monitoring, often driven by fear of being misunderstood or judged. The speaker may start a sentence, stop midway, and then change direction, which can make their communication appear disjointed or erratic.

Tone and Volume Shifts

Stress can also manifest through changes in tone and volume. These vocal shifts can reveal underlying emotions and provide clues about the intensity of the pressure someone is experiencing.

Raised or Tense Voice: When stressed, people often speak with a higher pitch or a strained tone. This tension in the voice can signal fear, frustration, or anxiety. For example, someone who feels cornered during a debate may respond with a raised voice, indicating their discomfort or defensive state. Rapid, loud bursts of speech can also reflect anger or desperation, while a trembling voice may betray fear or vulnerability.

Softened or Muted Voice: In contrast, stress can lead some individuals to speak more softly or mumble. This behavior may be a sign of insecurity, shame, or fear of confrontation. Lowering one's voice can also reflect an attempt to avoid drawing attention to oneself or to deflect further questioning. In high-stakes situations, such as interviews or difficult conversations, a muted tone can indicate a lack of confidence or reluctance to speak openly.

Word Choice and Language Patterns

The words people choose to use under stress often reveal their emotional state and coping mechanisms. Stress can lead to distinct changes in vocabulary, phrasing, and the way thoughts are expressed.

Vague or Ambiguous Language: People under stress may resort to vague or ambiguous language, avoiding specific details or commitments. This pattern can indicate a desire to deflect responsibility, minimize conflict, or evade difficult questions. For example, instead of providing a direct answer, a stressed individual might say, "I'm not sure" or "I'll get back to you," even when they have the information at hand.

Repetitive Speech: Repetition of certain phrases or ideas is another common pattern under stress. Repetition may reflect an effort to emphasize key points or to reassure oneself. For example, someone under scrutiny might repeatedly state, "I didn't do it" as a way to convince themselves and others of their innocence. Repetition can also serve as a coping mechanism, helping the speaker regain a sense of control over the conversation.

Negative or Catastrophic Language: Stress can lead to more negative or catastrophic language, where the speaker focuses on worst-case scenarios, expresses pessimism, or uses absolute terms like "always" and "never." This type of language indicates a heightened sense of threat or hopelessness and may reflect cognitive distortions common during high-pressure situations.

Defensive or Aggressive Language: When people feel threatened or stressed, they may adopt defensive or aggressive language to protect themselves. This can include making accusations, shifting blame, or using sarcastic or confrontational speech. For example, a person feeling cornered might say, "Why are you blaming me?" or "You never understand!" This language pattern reflects their attempt to regain control of the situation or redirect attention.

Non-Verbal Cues Accompanying Speech Patterns

The way people speak under stress is often accompanied by non-verbal cues that provide additional context to their communication.

Facial Expressions and Eye Contact: Stress can lead to tense facial muscles, forced smiles, or furrowed brows. Changes in eye contact, such as avoiding eye contact or rapidly shifting gaze, can also indicate discomfort. When someone looks down or away while speaking, it may reflect a lack of confidence or an attempt to hide their true feelings.

Gestures and Body Language: Stressed speakers may exhibit more frequent or erratic gestures, such as fidgeting, tapping, or wringing their hands. Conversely, they might become rigid, with limited movements and closed-off body language. These physical behaviors complement changes in speech patterns and help reveal the speaker's emotional state.

Contextual Considerations in Interpreting Stress-Related Speech Patterns

While stress-related speech patterns provide valuable clues about a person's emotional state, it is important to consider context when interpreting these cues. Not all signs of stress indicate dishonesty or conflict; some may reflect genuine anxiety, social discomfort, or situational pressures. Factors such as cultural norms, individual personality traits, and past experiences also play a role in how people express themselves under stress.

To accurately interpret speech patterns, it is helpful to establish a baseline for the person's typical behavior in low-stress situations. This allows for comparison and more accurate detection of deviations that may signal stress or pressure.

Jumping to conclusions based solely on changes in speech can lead to misunderstandings or unfair judgments. Instead, consider other verbal and non-verbal cues, ask clarifying questions, and take into account the broader context before making inferences about the person's state of mind.

Chapter Four: Appearance and What It Reveals

The choices we make regarding what to wear, how we style ourselves, and the way we carry ourselves are often influenced by culture, personal taste, social expectations, and even psychological factors. These aspects of self-presentation tell a story about who we are—or who we want to be perceived as—without the need for words.

Clothing as a Reflection of Identity

Clothing choices often reflect a person's identity, whether consciously or unconsciously. Fashion is one of the most visible markers of individual and group identity, and it communicates messages about social status, cultural belonging, gender, occupation, values, and even moods.

Cultural and Social Signifiers: Clothing is deeply rooted in culture and often conveys specific meanings within different social contexts. Traditional clothing, such as a kimono in Japan, a sari in India, or a suit and tie in Western business culture, reflects adherence to cultural norms and traditions. These garments carry historical, religious, or ritualistic significance that goes beyond aesthetics. Wearing such clothing can express pride in cultural heritage, respect for customs, or a desire to connect with a community.

Social groups also use fashion as a means of creating and reinforcing identity. Subcultures, such as goths, punks, or hip-hop enthusiasts, often adopt distinctive clothing styles that signal membership and shared values. These stylistic choices differentiate the group from mainstream society, serving as both an expression of individuality and a form of collective identity.

Status and Social Class: Clothing often reflects an individual's socioeconomic status. Luxury brands, designer labels, and tailored clothing can signify wealth, prestige, or social aspiration. Conversely, practical or modest attire may indicate a focus on functionality, resourcefulness, or resistance to consumerism. While these markers are not definitive—people may choose certain clothing to project an image that differs from their reality—fashion remains a common way to signal one's position within society.

Personal Style and Individuality: Many people use clothing to express their unique personality, tastes, and preferences. Choices in color, fabric, and style can reflect one's mood, creativity, or even political beliefs. Someone who consistently wears bright, bold colors may be seen as outgoing and confident, while someone who opts for minimalist, monochrome outfits may project a sense of order and professionalism. Personal style allows individuals to assert their identity, distinguish themselves from others, and communicate aspects of who they are without speaking.

Gender Identity and Self-Expression: Clothing and grooming choices are often closely linked to gender identity. For many, dressing in ways that align with their gender identity is a form of self-affirmation and authenticity. Transgender and non-binary individuals, for example, may use clothing to reflect their gender identity and feel more comfortable in their own skin. On the other hand, people who challenge traditional gender norms through androgynous or gender-fluid fashion may be expressing resistance to societal expectations and embracing a broader definition of identity.

Grooming as a Marker of Self-Image and Values

Grooming choices, such as hairstyles, facial hair, makeup, and overall hygiene, further convey aspects of identity, self-esteem, and social positioning. Grooming rituals vary widely across cultures and can serve as markers of tradition, rebellion, or personal care.

Hairstyles and Cultural Significance: Hairstyles often carry cultural and social significance. For example, in many Black communities, natural hairstyles like afros, dreadlocks, and braids represent pride, cultural identity, and resistance to Eurocentric beauty standards. Conversely, altering one's hair to fit mainstream norms—such as through straightening—may reflect a desire for social acceptance or the influence of societal pressures. In other contexts, specific hairstyles may indicate religious observance, such as the uncut hair and turbans worn by Sikh men or the shaved heads of Buddhist monks.

Makeup as Art and Expression: Makeup is another form of grooming that allows for self-expression. For some, makeup is a form of artistic creativity, enabling them to experiment with different looks and reflect their personality or mood. For others, it may serve as a mask, providing confidence or shielding vulnerabilities. The decision to wear makeup—or not—can communicate values, such as rejecting traditional beauty standards or embracing femininity.

Beards, Facial Hair, and Symbolism: Facial hair, such as beards or mustaches, can symbolize masculinity, tradition, rebellion, or identity. In some cultures, beards are a sign of maturity, wisdom, or religious observance, while in others, they may reflect a fashion trend. Grooming choices related to facial hair often carry deeper meanings tied to personal beliefs, social roles, and self-image.

Hygiene and Self-Care: Overall grooming and hygiene habits also reflect how individuals view themselves and their place in society. Well-groomed individuals may project an image of professionalism, self-respect, and attention to detail, while neglecting grooming can signal stress, depression, or a rejection of societal norms. Personal care routines, such as skin care, hair maintenance, or dental hygiene, often reflect cultural standards of beauty and health, as well as individual attitudes toward self-care.

Personal Presentation

Beyond clothing and grooming, personal presentation encompasses body language, posture, accessories, and overall demeanor. These elements communicate non-verbal messages about confidence, approachability, social roles, and internal states.

Posture and Confidence: Posture is a key aspect of personal presentation that conveys self-assurance or insecurity. An upright, open posture suggests confidence, approachability, and engagement, while slouched or closed-off body language can indicate shyness, insecurity, or disinterest. Posture often interacts with clothing and grooming to create a cohesive impression of who a person is and how they feel about themselves.

Accessories as Statements: Accessories—such as jewelry, watches, glasses, hats, and bags—also communicate identity. A luxury watch may signify wealth and status, while a handmade bracelet may represent personal values or affiliations. Accessories can reflect hobbies, beliefs, and social ties, serving as subtle cues that invite others to learn more about the wearer's identity.

Attire and Contextual Adaptation: The appropriateness of attire for different situations also plays a role in personal presentation. Dressing for a job interview, a wedding, or a casual gathering requires an understanding of social norms and expectations. How individuals adapt their clothing to fit these contexts demonstrates their social awareness, cultural sensitivity, and understanding of their role within a given setting.

The Complexity of Self-Expression Through Appearance

While clothing, grooming, and personal presentation often reveal aspects of identity, they can also be used to conceal, manipulate, or challenge perceptions. A person may dress conservatively for a job interview to appear more professional but express their true self through more relaxed attire outside of work. Similarly, individuals may use fashion as armor, projecting confidence to mask insecurity or choosing deliberately provocative styles to challenge norms and provoke thought.

It is important to remember that self-presentation is complex and influenced by factors such as culture, socioeconomic status, access to resources, and personal experiences. Judging someone solely by their appearance risks oversimplifying their identity and ignoring the layers of meaning behind their choices. To truly understand what clothing, grooming, and presentation reveal about a person, one must approach these signals with curiosity, empathy, and an awareness of context.

Identifying Personality Traits Through Personal Style

The clothing people choose to wear often reflects their core personality traits. While personal style can be influenced by cultural norms, trends, or practical considerations, it is also a form of self-expression that conveys unique aspects of who someone is.

Classic and Conservative Style: Individuals who favor classic, timeless pieces, such as tailored suits, simple dresses, neutral colors, and minimal accessories, often exhibit traits like reliability, discipline, and attention to detail. This style conveys professionalism, tradition, and a preference for stability and structure. People with a classic style may seek consistency in other areas of life and often appreciate order, predictability, and traditional values.

Bold and Eccentric Style: A bold, eclectic style characterized by bright colors, unique patterns, and unconventional combinations suggests creativity, confidence, and a willingness to stand out from the crowd. Individuals who embrace eccentric fashion often enjoy expressing their individuality and challenging social norms. This style reflects traits like open-mindedness, playfulness, and a desire for self-expression. People with bold style choices may be comfortable taking risks and exploring new ideas.

Casual and Comfortable Style: Those who prioritize comfort and practicality in their clothing—opting for casual jeans, t-shirts, and sneakers—often exhibit traits such as approachability, flexibility, and a laid-back attitude. This style can reflect a preference for simplicity and a focus on practicality over formality. People who favor casual clothing may value authenticity, down-to-earth interactions, and a relaxed lifestyle. They may also be seen as adaptable and easygoing in social situations.

Fashion-Forward and Trend-Conscious Style: Individuals who stay on top of fashion trends, frequently updating their wardrobe with the latest styles, often display traits like sociability, confidence, and a desire for recognition. This style suggests an awareness of social dynamics and a desire to make a positive impression. Trend-conscious people may seek social validation and enjoy the status associated with being fashionable. They often enjoy socializing and thrive in environments that offer opportunities to connect and be seen.

Minimalist Style: A minimalist style, characterized by clean lines, muted colors, and a lack of excess, often reflects traits like intentionality, focus, and a preference for simplicity. Individuals with a minimalist wardrobe may value quality over quantity and seek to remove clutter from both their wardrobe and their lives. This style often suggests a thoughtful, introspective personality and a desire to focus on what truly matters.

Accessories and Their Meanings

The accessories people choose—such as jewelry, watches, bags, and hats—offer further clues about their personality traits, values, and priorities.

Statement Jewelry and Bold Accessories: Wearing bold, eye-catching jewelry or unique accessories often signals a confident, expressive personality. People who choose these items may enjoy drawing attention, showcasing their individuality, and engaging in social interactions. This choice reflects a desire to make a lasting impression and to use fashion as a form of self-expression and conversation.

Minimalist and Subtle Accessories: Individuals who wear minimalist or subtle accessories, such as a simple watch or understated earrings, often convey a sense of restraint, elegance, and intentionality. This style suggests traits like conscientiousness, focus, and a preference for understated sophistication. Such individuals may prioritize function and meaning over showiness, reflecting an appreciation for quality and purposeful choices.

Cultural or Symbolic Accessories: Wearing accessories that have cultural or symbolic significance, such as religious symbols, family heirlooms, or items with personal meaning, often reflects a strong connection to identity, tradition, and values. These individuals may prioritize heritage, spirituality, or community ties, and their accessories serve as meaningful extensions of their beliefs and experiences.

High-End and Designer Accessories: Opting for luxury and designer accessories often indicates traits such as ambition, status-consciousness, or a desire for recognition. People who favor high-end items may appreciate the craftsmanship and prestige associated with these brands. This style can reflect a drive for success, social validation, or a preference for the finer things in life.

Grooming Habits and Personality Insights

Personal grooming habits—including hairstyles, makeup, and overall hygiene—offer further insights into personality traits, self-esteem, and social attitudes.

Meticulous Grooming: Individuals who consistently present themselves with meticulous grooming, carefully styled hair, and flawless makeup often exhibit traits like discipline, conscientiousness, and attention to detail. This level of grooming suggests a desire to make a strong impression, maintain control over one's appearance, and uphold a polished image. Such individuals may take pride in their achievements, seek approval, or adhere to high standards of self-care.

Natural or Minimal Grooming: A preference for a natural or minimal grooming routine often reflects traits like authenticity, practicality, and confidence in one's natural appearance. These individuals may prioritize inner qualities over outward appearances and prefer a no-fuss approach to personal care. Natural grooming can signal a strong sense of self-worth and a desire to be seen as genuine and approachable.

Bold Hair Colors and Creative Makeup: Experimenting with bold hair colors, dramatic makeup, or creative styles often indicates traits like creativity, openness, and a desire for self-expression. Individuals who embrace these looks may enjoy standing out, challenging norms, and expressing their artistic side. This type of grooming reflects a willingness to take risks and explore new forms of self-expression.

Casual and Low-Maintenance Grooming: People who adopt a low-maintenance grooming routine, such as a simple hairstyle or minimal makeup, often prioritize practicality and comfort. This choice suggests traits like adaptability, independence, and a focus on inner values over outward appearances. Such individuals may be easygoing, down-to-earth, and less concerned with external validation.

Personal Presentation as a Form of Self-Expression

Personal style extends beyond clothing and grooming to include posture, body language, and overall demeanor. How individuals carry themselves often reflects their confidence, approachability, and social attitudes.

Confident and Open Posture: A confident posture, characterized by an upright stance, relaxed shoulders, and direct eye contact, often signals self-assurance, assertiveness, and a willingness to engage. People with open body language are often perceived as approachable, friendly, and trustworthy.

Reserved and Closed-Off Body Language: Conversely, individuals with reserved or closed-off body language—such as crossed arms, hunched shoulders, or avoiding eye contact—may be shy, introspective, or cautious. This posture can indicate a desire to protect oneself, social anxiety, or simply a preference for introspection and solitude.

Expressive Gestures: Using expressive gestures while speaking often reflects traits like enthusiasm, passion, and energy. Individuals who gesture frequently may be highly communicative, emotionally attuned, and comfortable expressing themselves. This trait is often seen in extroverted, socially engaged individuals.

Recognizing Cultural and Socioeconomic Indicators

Culture encompasses shared beliefs, values, customs, traditions, language, and behaviors that define a group of people. Recognizing cultural indicators requires an understanding of the elements that make up different cultures and how they influence the ways people live, communicate, and interact.

Language and Communication Styles: Language is one of the most visible markers of culture. The language people speak, the phrases they use, and even the tone and style of their communication reflect cultural influences. Some cultures prioritize direct communication, while others value indirect and nuanced speech. For example, Western cultures often favor assertiveness and clarity, while East Asian cultures may emphasize harmony and indirectness. Recognizing these communication styles can prevent misunderstandings and facilitate more effective interactions.

Cultural norms also influence non-verbal communication, such as body language, eye contact, and gestures. In some cultures, maintaining eye contact shows respect and confidence; in others, it may be considered rude or disrespectful. Similarly, gestures that are positive or neutral in one culture may carry different or even offensive meanings in another.

Traditions and Customs: Cultural traditions and customs play a significant role in shaping behavior, dress, celebrations, and rituals. For example, religious observances, such as Ramadan for Muslims or Passover for Jews, influence daily routines, dietary habits, and social practices. Understanding these traditions fosters respect and empathy, particularly when interacting with individuals from different cultural backgrounds.

Attire and Appearance: Clothing, hairstyles, and grooming choices often reflect cultural norms, beliefs, and traditions. For example, wearing a hijab, turban, or kippah can indicate religious or cultural observance. Traditional attire, such as a kimono in Japan or an embroidered dress in Eastern Europe, may be worn to express cultural pride, honor special occasions, or adhere to traditional customs. Recognizing the significance of these expressions of identity helps avoid superficial judgments based solely on appearance.

Values and Beliefs: Cultural values shape how people view concepts such as family, individualism, community, gender roles, and authority. For instance, collectivist cultures often prioritize group harmony and interdependence, while individualist cultures emphasize personal achievement and autonomy. Recognizing these values can help explain behaviors that might seem unfamiliar or contradictory through a different cultural lens.

Symbols and Rituals: Symbols, rituals, and practices often carry deep meaning within cultures. From national symbols, like flags and emblems, to sacred rituals, such as weddings, funerals, or rites of passage, these elements reflect the identity and shared history of a group. Observing and understanding these symbols can provide insights into what a culture values and how individuals see themselves within that culture.

Identifying Socioeconomic Indicators

Socioeconomic status (SES) reflects an individual's economic and social position within a society, based on factors such as income, education, occupation, and access to resources. Socioeconomic indicators impact lifestyle, opportunities, and even perceptions of success or worth.

Clothing, Accessories, and Material Possessions: Clothing and possessions often reflect socioeconomic status. Designer brands, expensive accessories, and high-end technology can signal wealth and access to resources.

Conversely, practical, second-hand, or utilitarian clothing may reflect limited financial means. However, it is crucial to avoid making assumptions solely based on outward appearances, as individuals may adopt specific styles for cultural, personal, or environmental reasons unrelated to SES.

Speech and Language Patterns: Socioeconomic background can influence how people speak, including their vocabulary, accent, and even the topics they discuss. Educational background often shapes language use, with individuals from higher socioeconomic backgrounds frequently exposed to different language norms, expressions, and jargon. Recognizing these differences can help avoid stereotyping and foster more inclusive communication.

Educational Attainment and Occupation: Access to education is a key determinant of socioeconomic status. Higher levels of education often correlate with greater economic opportunities and social mobility. Recognizing the level of education a person has received can provide insight into their perspectives, experiences, and professional opportunities. Similarly, occupation and employment status often reflect socioeconomic positioning. A professional working in a high-income, specialized field may have different social and economic concerns than someone in a lower-paying, precarious job.

Living Conditions and Lifestyle: Socioeconomic status can also be seen through a person's living conditions and lifestyle choices. Access to safe housing, healthcare, nutritious food, and recreational activities often depends on one's financial means. People from lower socioeconomic backgrounds may face challenges related to basic needs, such as food security or healthcare access, which can impact behavior and outlook. Recognizing these indicators fosters empathy and highlights the need to consider systemic factors that shape individual lives.

Access to Opportunities and Mobility: Socioeconomic background influences access to opportunities, such as higher education, professional advancement, or networking connections. Those from wealthier backgrounds may have more social capital, mentorship opportunities, and institutional support, while those from less privileged backgrounds may face systemic barriers that hinder mobility. Recognizing this disparity is essential for creating equitable environments and reducing bias in social, educational, and professional settings.

The Intersection of Culture and Socioeconomic Status

Cultural and socioeconomic indicators often intersect, shaping an individual's identity and experiences in complex ways. For example, within the same cultural group, people may experience vastly different opportunities and challenges based on their socioeconomic status. A wealthy individual and a low-income individual from the same cultural background may express their identity differently, navigate social norms differently, and have divergent perspectives on issues like education, work, and healthcare.

Stereotypes and Biases: Recognizing cultural and socioeconomic indicators requires sensitivity to avoid reinforcing stereotypes and biases. Making assumptions based solely on someone's clothing, speech, or living conditions can lead to unfair judgments and perpetuate harmful narratives. Instead, it is important to view these indicators as starting points for deeper understanding and empathy, rather than definitive markers of identity or worth.

Empathy and Respect: The goal of recognizing cultural and socioeconomic indicators is to foster empathy, bridge differences, and promote respect. Understanding these indicators allows us to appreciate diverse experiences, communicate more effectively, and create inclusive environments that honor each person's unique background and perspective.

Chapter Five: Personality Traits and Psychological Profiling

Key Personality Frameworks

Personality frameworks provide valuable tools for understanding human behavior, motivations, and individual differences. By categorizing personality traits and tendencies, these models offer insights into how people think, feel, and interact with the world around them. Two of the most widely used and researched frameworks are the Big Five Personality Traits (also known as the Five-Factor Model) and the Myers-Briggs Type Indicator (MBTI). Each of these models approaches personality in different ways, with its own strengths, limitations, and practical applications. In addition, there are several other notable frameworks, such as the Enneagram and DISC, that offer additional perspectives on personality.

The Big Five Personality Traits (Five-Factor Model)

The Big Five Personality Traits are considered the gold standard in personality psychology due to their strong empirical support and cross-cultural applicability. This model proposes that personality can be described based on five broad dimensions, each of which captures a range of traits and behaviors:

1. **Openness to Experience**: Openness describes a person's willingness to embrace new ideas, experiences,

and change. High levels of openness are associated with creativity, curiosity, and a preference for novelty and variety. People with low openness tend to be more conventional, practical, and resistant to change.

Key Characteristics:

- High Openness: Imaginative, curious, open-minded, artistic, and adventurous.

- Low Openness: Practical, traditional, routine-oriented, and conservative.

2. Conscientiousness: Conscientiousness reflects a person's degree of organization, responsibility, and dependability. Highly conscientious individuals are often disciplined, goal-oriented, and detail-oriented. Those with lower conscientiousness may be more spontaneous, flexible, or prone to procrastination.

Key Characteristics:

- High Conscientiousness: Organized, reliable, disciplined, and hardworking.

- Low Conscientiousness: Carefree, disorganized, impulsive, and less goal-oriented.

3. Extraversion: Extraversion measures a person's sociability, energy level, and tendency to seek stimulation from external sources. Extroverts are outgoing, talkative, and energized by social interactions, while introverts tend to be more reserved, introspective, and comfortable with solitude.

Key Characteristics:

- High Extraversion: Sociable, energetic, assertive, and enthusiastic.

- Low Extraversion (Introversion): Reserved, thoughtful, quiet, and independent.

4. Agreeableness: Agreeableness captures a person's tendency to be cooperative, compassionate, and trusting in interactions with others. Highly agreeable individuals prioritize social harmony and are often empathetic and kind. Those low in agreeableness may be more competitive, skeptical, or blunt.

Key Characteristics:

- High Agreeableness: Friendly, empathetic, cooperative, and supportive.

- Low Agreeableness: Competitive, critical, uncooperative, and independent-minded.

5. Neuroticism: Neuroticism refers to emotional stability and resilience to stress. High neuroticism indicates a tendency to experience negative emotions, such as anxiety, sadness, or irritability. Low neuroticism suggests greater emotional stability and an ability to remain calm under pressure.

Key Characteristics:

- High Neuroticism: Anxious, moody, self-conscious, and emotionally reactive.

- Low Neuroticism (Emotional Stability): Calm, resilient, secure, and emotionally stable.

The Big Five model is often used in research, workplace settings, and personal development to understand individual differences, predict behavior, and improve communication. Its strength lies in its ability to capture a broad range of personality traits with strong predictive validity.

The Myers-Briggs Type Indicator (MBTI)

The Myers-Briggs Type Indicator (MBTI) is one of the most popular personality frameworks used in both personal and professional contexts. Developed by Isabel Briggs Myers and Katharine Cook Briggs, the MBTI categorizes individuals into 16 personality types based on preferences in four dichotomous dimensions:

1. **Extraversion (E) vs. Introversion (I)**: This dimension describes where individuals prefer to focus their energy and attention. Extraverts are energized by social interactions and external stimulation, while introverts prefer reflection, solitude, and smaller social settings.

2. **Sensing (S) vs. Intuition (N)**: This dichotomy focuses on how people perceive and gather information. Sensing individuals prefer concrete, factual, and sensory information, while intuitive individuals focus on patterns, possibilities, and abstract concepts.

3. **Thinking (T) vs. Feeling (F)**: This dimension relates to decision-making and how individuals prioritize values. Thinking types prioritize logic, analysis, and objectivity,

while feeling types prioritize empathy, values, and personal considerations.

4. Judging (J) vs. Perceiving (P): This dimension describes how people approach structure and organization. Judging types prefer planning, decisiveness, and structured environments, while perceiving types prefer flexibility, spontaneity, and adaptability.

The MBTI combines these preferences into 16 personality types, such as INFJ (Introversion, Intuition, Feeling, Judging) or ESTP (Extraversion, Sensing, Thinking, Perceiving). Each type is associated with distinct strengths, weaknesses, and preferences in communication, problem-solving, and relationships.

Other Notable Personality Frameworks

In addition to the Big Five and MBTI, several other frameworks offer unique perspectives on personality:

The Enneagram: The Enneagram is a personality model that divides individuals into nine core types, each with its own motivations, fears, and behavior patterns. The nine types are often described as: Reformer (Type 1), Helper (Type 2), Achiever (Type 3), Individualist (Type 4), Investigator (Type 5), Loyalist (Type 6), Enthusiast (Type 7), Challenger (Type 8), and Peacemaker (Type 9). Each type is interconnected, and individuals may exhibit traits from neighboring types (known as "wings"). The Enneagram focuses on self-awareness, growth, and transformation, making it popular in personal development and counseling.

DISC Model: The DISC model categorizes personality into four primary types: Dominance (D), Influence (I), Steadiness (S), and Conscientiousness (C). It is often used in workplace settings to improve communication, teamwork, and leadership. The model focuses on behavioral tendencies and how individuals respond to challenges, people, pace, and procedures.

Holland's Career Typology (RIASEC): This model, developed by psychologist John Holland, classifies individuals into six career-oriented types: Realistic, Investigative, Artistic, Social, Enterprising, and Conventional (RIASEC). It is commonly used in career counseling to match individuals with occupations that align with their interests and personality traits.

Jungian Archetypes: Carl Jung's archetypes are symbolic images and patterns that represent universal human experiences. Jung identified several archetypes, such as the Hero, the Caregiver, the Explorer, and the Shadow. These archetypes provide insight into unconscious motivations and recurring themes in behavior.

Recognizing Introversion, Extroversion, and Other Major Traits

Understanding personality traits, particularly those related to introversion, extroversion, and other key dimensions, provides valuable insights into how people engage with the world, process information, and interact with others. While no single trait fully defines an individual, recognizing major traits can enhance self-awareness, improve relationships, and facilitate more effective communication.

Introversion and Extroversion: Two Ends of the Spectrum

Introversion and extroversion are foundational personality traits first popularized by psychologist Carl Jung and later incorporated into numerous personality frameworks, including the Myers-Briggs Type Indicator (MBTI) and the Big Five Personality Traits model. These traits describe where individuals draw their energy from and how they prefer to engage with their environment and others.

Introversion

Introverts tend to be energized by solitude and require time alone to recharge after social interactions. They often prefer deep, meaningful conversations over small talk and may feel drained by prolonged socializing or large gatherings. Introverts typically focus on internal thoughts, feelings, and observations, and they may be more reflective, reserved, and detail-oriented.

Common Traits of Introverts:

- Prefer solitary activities or small groups over large gatherings.

- Value quiet, reflective environments for work and leisure.

- May be more sensitive to external stimuli, such as noise and light.

- Enjoy deep and focused conversations.

- Take time to process thoughts before speaking or making decisions.

Recognizing Introversion:: An introvert may appear quiet, thoughtful, or reserved in social settings. They are often good listeners and may contribute thoughtful, well-considered ideas rather than speaking impulsively. Introverts may seek out alone time after social interactions to recharge and reflect, and they are often comfortable working independently or in quiet settings.

Extroversion

Extroverts are energized by social interactions and external stimulation. They thrive in dynamic, people-oriented environments and often enjoy being the center of attention. Extroverts tend to be outgoing, talkative, and enthusiastic, drawing energy from engaging with others. They often enjoy collaborative work, group activities, and high-energy social settings.

Common Traits of Extroverts:

- Enjoy socializing and connecting with new people.

- Prefer group activities and teamwork.

- May act quickly and adapt to changing circumstances.

- Feel energized by external stimulation, such as crowds or events.

- Communicate openly and assertively.

Recognizing Extroversion: Extroverts often initiate conversations, introduce themselves to new people, and seek out opportunities for social interaction. They may speak quickly, share personal stories or jokes, and enjoy participating in group discussions or activities. Extroverts often display enthusiasm and are comfortable with spontaneous situations or new experiences.

The Introversion-Extroversion Spectrum: It is important to note that introversion and extroversion exist on a spectrum. Many people fall somewhere in between, displaying traits of both sides depending on the context. These individuals are often referred to as "ambiverts." Ambiverts may enjoy socializing but also value time alone, striking a balance between external stimulation and introspection.

Other Major Personality Traits and How to Recognize Them

In addition to introversion and extroversion, several other major traits play a key role in shaping personality. These traits, often captured in the Big Five Personality Traits model, help explain individual differences in behavior, thought processes, and emotional responses.

1. Openness to Experience: Openness describes a person's willingness to engage with new ideas, experiences, and unconventional perspectives. Highly open individuals are curious, imaginative, and creative, while those low in openness may prefer routine, practicality, and familiarity.

Recognizing Openness:

- High Openness: Creative pursuits, diverse interests, willingness to try new things, appreciation for art and abstract ideas, and curiosity about unfamiliar concepts.

- Low Openness: Preference for tradition and routine, practical decision-making, focus on concrete details, and skepticism of new or unconventional ideas.

2. Conscientiousness: Conscientiousness reflects an individual's level of organization, responsibility, and attention to detail. Highly conscientious people are disciplined, goal-oriented, and reliable, while those lower in conscientiousness may be more spontaneous or flexible, sometimes bordering on disorganization.

Recognizing Conscientiousness:

- High Conscientiousness: Punctuality, meticulous planning, strong work ethic, attention to detail, and a methodical approach to tasks.

- Low Conscientiousness: Flexibility, spontaneity, tendency to procrastinate, and a more relaxed approach to deadlines and organization.

3. Agreeableness: Agreeableness describes a person's tendency to be compassionate, cooperative, and trusting. Highly agreeable individuals are often empathetic and enjoy helping others, while those low in agreeableness may be more competitive, critical, or skeptical.

Recognizing Agreeableness:

- High Agreeableness: Friendly demeanor, willingness to compromise, active listening, showing empathy, and building harmonious relationships.

- Low Agreeableness: Competitive nature, blunt communication style, tendency to challenge ideas, and a focus on self-interest or independence.

4. Neuroticism (Emotional Stability): Neuroticism reflects emotional stability and resilience to stress. Individuals high in neuroticism are more likely to experience negative emotions such as anxiety, anger, or sadness, while those low in neuroticism tend to be calm, composed, and emotionally resilient.

Recognizing Neuroticism:

- High Neuroticism: Frequent worry, mood swings, self-doubt, and sensitivity to stress or criticism.

- Low Neuroticism (Emotionally Stable): Calm demeanor, resilience to stress, consistent mood, and lower reactivity to negative events.

Why Recognizing Personality Traits Matters

Recognizing personality traits, such as introversion, extroversion, and others, enhances our understanding of human behavior and improves our ability to communicate, collaborate, and build meaningful relationships. Awareness of these traits helps to:

- **Improve Communication:** Tailoring communication styles based on a person's traits—such as providing more time for an introvert to reflect before responding or engaging an extrovert in lively discussion—can lead to more effective and meaningful interactions.

- **Foster Empathy and Acceptance:** Recognizing and appreciating personality differences reduces the likelihood of misunderstanding and judgment, promoting greater empathy and respect for individual preferences and needs.

- **Enhance Teamwork and Leadership:** Understanding personality traits can improve teamwork by aligning roles and tasks with individuals' strengths and preferences. Leaders can better motivate and support their team by recognizing each person's unique traits.

Psychological Disorders and Their Behavioral Markers

While personality traits like introversion and extroversion describe enduring patterns of behavior and preference, psychological disorders involve disruptions in thoughts, emotions, and behaviors that can significantly impair an individual's ability to function in daily life. Each disorder has its own unique set of behavioral markers and symptoms, which can vary in intensity and expression.

Anxiety Disorders and Their Behavioral Markers

Anxiety disorders are characterized by excessive fear, worry, or nervousness that interferes with daily activities. Common types of anxiety disorders include generalized anxiety disorder (GAD), social anxiety disorder, panic disorder, and specific phobias.

Generalized Anxiety Disorder (GAD): GAD involves chronic, excessive worry about various aspects of life, such as work, relationships, health, or everyday tasks.

Behavioral Markers:

- Constant worry, even about minor or everyday situations.

- Difficulty concentrating or a sense of mind going blank.

- Restlessness, feeling "on edge," or irritability.

- Physical symptoms such as muscle tension, headaches, stomachaches, or fatigue.

- Avoidance of situations that may trigger anxiety.

Social Anxiety Disorder: Social anxiety disorder involves an intense fear of social situations due to concerns about being judged, embarrassed, or humiliated.

Behavioral Markers:

- Avoidance of social interactions, public speaking, or situations involving unfamiliar people.

- Intense fear or discomfort in social settings.

- Difficulty making eye contact or engaging in conversations.

- Sweating, trembling, blushing, or other signs of physical distress in social situations.

Panic Disorder: Panic disorder is marked by recurring and unexpected panic attacks—sudden episodes of intense fear or discomfort.

Behavioral Markers:

- Sudden onset of intense fear, often accompanied by a racing heart, shortness of breath, dizziness, or a sense of impending doom.

- Avoidance of places or situations where previous panic attacks occurred.

- Fear of losing control or dying during an attack.

Mood Disorders and Their Behavioral Markers

Mood disorders involve disturbances in a person's emotional state, leading to prolonged periods of extreme sadness, elevated mood, or both. Common mood disorders include major depressive disorder and bipolar disorder.

Major Depressive Disorder (Depression): Depression is characterized by persistent feelings of sadness, hopelessness, and a lack of interest or pleasure in daily activities.

Behavioral Markers:

- Persistent sadness, tearfulness, or irritability.

- Loss of interest in activities once enjoyed, including hobbies or socializing.

- Fatigue, low energy, or difficulty getting out of bed.

- Changes in appetite or weight (either loss or gain).

- Difficulty concentrating, making decisions, or experiencing feelings of worthlessness or guilt.

- Suicidal thoughts or behaviors in severe cases.

Bipolar Disorder: Bipolar disorder involves extreme mood swings that include episodes of mania (high energy and elevated mood) and depression (low energy and sadness).

Behavioral Markers:

- During manic episodes: heightened energy, reduced need for sleep, grandiosity, impulsive decision-making, excessive talking, or engaging in risky behaviors.

- During depressive episodes: symptoms similar to major depressive disorder, including sadness, fatigue, and loss of interest.

- Rapid shifts between mood states or prolonged periods in either the manic or depressive state.

Personality Disorders and Their Behavioral Markers

Personality disorders involve enduring patterns of behavior, cognition, and inner experience that deviate significantly from cultural norms. These patterns are pervasive and inflexible, affecting social, occupational, and relational functioning. Examples include borderline personality disorder (BPD), narcissistic personality disorder (NPD), and antisocial personality disorder (ASPD).

Borderline Personality Disorder (BPD): BPD is characterized by intense emotional instability, fear of abandonment, and difficulty maintaining stable relationships.

Behavioral Markers:

- Intense, unstable relationships with frequent shifts from idealization to devaluation.

- Fear of abandonment and frantic efforts to avoid real or imagined abandonment.

- Rapid mood swings and intense emotional reactions.

- Impulsive behaviors (e.g., spending sprees, substance abuse, self-harm).

- Chronic feelings of emptiness or unstable self-image.

Narcissistic Personality Disorder (NPD): NPD involves a pervasive pattern of grandiosity, need for admiration, and lack of empathy for others.

Behavioral Markers:

- Inflated sense of self-importance or superiority.

- Preoccupation with fantasies of success, power, or attractiveness.

- Need for excessive admiration and difficulty handling criticism.

- Exploiting others for personal gain.

- Lack of empathy and inability to recognize or care about the needs of others.

Antisocial Personality Disorder (ASPD): ASPD is characterized by a disregard for the rights of others, impulsivity, and a pattern of irresponsible or unlawful behavior.

Behavioral Markers:

- Frequent lying, deceitfulness, or manipulation.

- Disregard for social norms and laws, leading to criminal behavior.

- Lack of remorse or empathy for harming others.

- Impulsivity, irritability, and aggressiveness.

- Difficulty maintaining stable employment or relationships.

Psychotic Disorders and Their Behavioral Markers

Psychotic disorders, such as schizophrenia, involve a loss of contact with reality, often characterized by delusions, hallucinations, and disorganized thinking.

Schizophrenia

Schizophrenia is a chronic disorder that affects how a person thinks, feels, and behaves.

Behavioral Markers:

- Delusions (false beliefs that are resistant to reason or evidence).

- Hallucinations (perceptions of stimuli that are not present, such as hearing voices).

- Disorganized speech or thought processes, making communication difficult to follow.

- Flat affect (reduced emotional expression) or inappropriate emotional responses.

- Withdrawal from social interactions and lack of motivation.

Obsessive-Compulsive and Related Disorders

Obsessive-compulsive disorder (OCD) involves persistent, unwanted thoughts (obsessions) and repetitive behaviors (compulsions) performed to reduce anxiety.

Obsessive-Compulsive Disorder (OCD): OCD is characterized by obsessions (intrusive, unwanted thoughts) and compulsions (repetitive behaviors performed to alleviate distress).

Behavioral Markers:

- Repetitive rituals, such as excessive handwashing, checking locks, or counting.

- Avoidance of situations that trigger obsessions.

- Difficulty controlling or stopping compulsive behaviors despite knowing they are irrational.

- Distress or anxiety when unable to perform compulsions.

Neurodevelopmental and Neurocognitive Disorders

Neurodevelopmental disorders, such as autism spectrum disorder (ASD) and attention deficit hyperactivity disorder (ADHD), emerge in childhood and can impact social, academic, and cognitive functioning. Neurocognitive disorders, like dementia, often affect memory, cognition, and behavior later in life.

Autism Spectrum Disorder (ASD): ASD involves challenges in social communication, restricted interests, and repetitive behaviors.

Behavioral Markers:

- Difficulty with social interactions, such as making eye contact or understanding social cues.

- Restricted or repetitive behaviors, such as repetitive movements or adherence to routines.

- Intense focus on specific interests.

- Sensory sensitivities (e.g., heightened response to sounds, textures, or lights).

Attention Deficit Hyperactivity Disorder (ADHD): ADHD is characterized by patterns of inattention, hyperactivity, and impulsivity.

Behavioral Markers:

- Difficulty sustaining attention or following through on tasks.

- Impulsivity, such as interrupting others or acting without thinking.

- Restlessness, fidgeting, or an inability to sit still.

- Difficulty organizing tasks and managing time.

Chapter Six: Emotional Reactions and Triggers

Identifying Common Emotional Triggers

Emotional triggers are stimuli—events, situations, or interactions—that provoke strong emotional reactions, often out of proportion to the immediate context. These triggers can lead to feelings such as anger, anxiety, sadness, or frustration and are usually linked to past experiences, beliefs, or deeply held values. By identifying common emotional triggers, individuals can better understand their reactions, manage their emotions, and improve their relationships and interactions with others. Awareness of emotional triggers also promotes empathy, as it helps us recognize the potential sensitivities of those around us.

Triggers Related to Personal Identity and Self-Esteem

Many emotional triggers are tied to how we perceive ourselves and how we believe others see us. Threats to self-esteem, confidence, or identity often evoke strong emotional responses.

Criticism and Judgment: Receiving criticism, even if constructive, can trigger feelings of inadequacy, defensiveness, or hurt. For individuals with low self-esteem or a history of harsh judgment, criticism may evoke shame, anger, or anxiety. These feelings often stem from past experiences where criticism was equated with rejection, failure, or a lack of worth.

Rejection and Exclusion: Rejection, whether in romantic relationships, friendships, or professional settings, is a powerful emotional trigger. Feelings of rejection tap into our primal need for belonging and acceptance. Being excluded from a group, ignored by peers, or turned down in a personal relationship can trigger feelings of loneliness, sadness, or even unworthiness.

Failure and Perceived Inadequacy: Failing at a task or falling short of one's expectations can evoke feelings of inadequacy, guilt, or self-criticism. For individuals who tie their self-worth to achievement, perceived failure may be particularly triggering. This trigger often leads to self-doubt, fear of judgment, and anxiety about trying again.

Comparison to Others: Comparing oneself to others can lead to feelings of envy, inadequacy, or insecurity. Social media, where people often present curated highlights of their lives, can exacerbate these feelings. This trigger is rooted in a fear of not measuring up, being left behind, or feeling "less than" in comparison to peers.

Triggers Related to Control and Safety

A sense of control over our lives and environments is crucial to emotional well-being. When that sense of control is threatened, it can trigger intense emotional responses.

Loss of Control: Situations that lead to feelings of helplessness or loss of control can trigger anxiety, anger, or panic. Examples include sudden changes in plans, unexpected events, or feeling trapped in a situation with limited options. This trigger may be especially pronounced in individuals who have experienced trauma or abuse, where control was taken away.

Being Ignored or Overlooked: Feeling dismissed, overlooked, or ignored can evoke frustration, sadness, or anger. When people feel that their voice is unheard or their contributions are undervalued, it can threaten their sense of importance and agency. This trigger may be rooted in past experiences where someone felt invisible or devalued.

Uncertainty and Ambiguity: Situations involving ambiguity, uncertainty, or lack of clarity can be highly triggering for some individuals. The inability to predict outcomes or control events can lead to feelings of anxiety, insecurity, or dread. This trigger is often tied to a desire for stability, security, and predictability.

Triggers Related to Relationships and Boundaries

Emotional triggers often emerge within the context of relationships, where boundaries, expectations, and communication patterns can evoke strong emotional reactions.

Betrayal or Broken Trust: Experiencing betrayal—whether through infidelity, dishonesty, or a breach of trust—can trigger intense feelings of hurt, anger, and loss. Trust is fundamental to healthy relationships, and when it is broken, it can evoke a deep sense of vulnerability and betrayal rooted in past experiences.

Disrespect and Dismissiveness: Feeling disrespected, belittled, or dismissed can trigger anger, defensiveness, or hurt. This reaction may stem from a strong sense of self-respect or past experiences where one's dignity was undermined. Disrespect can take many forms, from condescending remarks to outright insults.

Violation of Personal Boundaries: When others encroach on one's personal, emotional, or physical boundaries, it can trigger feelings of discomfort, anger, or fear. People who have experienced boundary violations in the past, such as trauma survivors, may be particularly sensitive to this trigger. Establishing and respecting boundaries is essential for emotional safety and well-being.

Feeling Unappreciated or Taken for Granted: In relationships, feeling unappreciated or taken for granted can lead to resentment, sadness, or anger. This trigger often arises when people give a great deal of themselves—whether in work, caregiving, or relationships—and feel their efforts are unnoticed or undervalued.

Triggers Related to Past Trauma and Negative Experiences

Emotional triggers are often linked to past traumatic or painful experiences. Certain sights, sounds, words, or situations can evoke memories of past events, leading to intense emotional responses.

Flashbacks and Reminders of Trauma: For trauma survivors, specific stimuli—such as a smell, place, or sound—can trigger flashbacks or intense emotional reactions. These triggers are often unpredictable and may lead to feelings of fear, helplessness, or distress, as if the trauma is happening again.

Abandonment or Neglect: Past experiences of abandonment or neglect, especially during childhood, can make individuals highly sensitive to situations where they feel unsupported or unloved. This trigger may manifest as fear of being left alone, anxiety in relationships, or difficulty trusting others.

Unresolved Grief: Losses that have not been fully processed or mourned can resurface when triggered by reminders of the person or situation. For example, an anniversary of a loved one's death, hearing a song, or visiting a particular place may evoke intense feelings of grief and sadness.

Triggers Related to Values and Beliefs

Emotional triggers are often tied to deeply held values and beliefs. When these values are challenged, ignored, or dismissed, it can lead to strong emotional reactions.

Moral Violations: Encountering behavior or actions that go against one's moral or ethical beliefs can trigger anger, disgust, or frustration. For example, witnessing acts of cruelty, injustice, or dishonesty may evoke strong emotional responses, especially for individuals with a strong moral compass.

Injustice and Unfair Treatment: Being treated unfairly, witnessing discrimination, or seeing others treated unjustly can trigger intense feelings of anger, sadness, or helplessness. This trigger often stems from a desire for fairness, equality, and justice in one's interactions and society at large.

Challenges to Identity or Beliefs: When a person's core beliefs, values, or identity are questioned or attacked, it can evoke defensive reactions, anger, or anxiety. This trigger is common in discussions of politics, religion, culture, or deeply held personal convictions.

Predicting Behavior Based on Emotional Responses

Our emotional responses influence how we think, make decisions, and interact with others. By understanding and predicting behavior based on these emotional responses, we can gain insight into what drives people's actions, how they cope with challenges, and how they navigate social dynamics. Emotions such as fear, anger, joy, sadness, and surprise often act as catalysts for specific behaviors, shaping our reactions to situations and guiding our choices.

How Emotions Influence Behavior

Emotions are complex reactions that involve physiological, cognitive, and behavioral components. When triggered, emotions serve as a signal that prompts a person to act in a way that addresses the perceived threat, reward, or challenge. For example, fear may lead to avoidance or protective behavior, while joy may prompt social connection and positive engagement.

Fight, Flight, or Freeze Response (Fear and Anxiety): When faced with perceived danger, fear triggers the body's fight, flight, or freeze response. This automatic response aims to protect the individual from harm. The behavioral outcomes of this emotional state can vary based on the individual and context:

- **Flight Behavior:** Some people may avoid the source of their fear entirely, whether by leaving a room, withdrawing from a confrontation, or steering clear of situations that provoke anxiety.

- **Fight Behavior:** Others may confront the source of their fear with assertiveness, aggression, or attempts to regain control.

- **Freeze Behavior:** In some cases, individuals may become immobilized, unable to act due to overwhelming fear or anxiety.

By recognizing how someone responds to fear or anxiety, we can better predict their behavior in stressful situations, offer appropriate support, or design interventions to help them manage their emotions.

Anger and Assertive or Aggressive Behavior: Anger is an emotional response to perceived injustice, threat, or frustration. It often serves as a motivating force for taking action to address a wrong, regain control, or defend oneself. However, the way anger manifests varies widely:

- **Constructive Assertion:** For some individuals, anger can lead to assertive communication, such as calmly but firmly stating their needs or setting boundaries.

- **Aggression:** Others may react with hostility, physical confrontation, or verbal outbursts.

- **Passive-Aggression:** Alternatively, individuals may express their anger indirectly through sarcastic comments, procrastination, or subtle acts of defiance.

Understanding the triggers and patterns of an individual's anger can help predict whether they will engage in constructive problem-solving, confrontation, or passive resistance when faced with conflict.

Sadness and Withdrawal or Help-Seeking Behavior: Sadness is often associated with loss, disappointment, or unmet needs. This emotional state can lead to a range of behaviors that reflect an attempt to cope with or alleviate the pain:

- **Withdrawal and Isolation:** Some people may withdraw from social interactions, preferring solitude to process their emotions. This behavior may be a coping mechanism to protect themselves from further hurt or to find space for introspection.

- **Help-Seeking:** Others may reach out to friends, family, or professionals for emotional support. Help-seeking behavior is often influenced by personality traits, social support networks, and past experiences.

- **Reflective or Creative Expression:** In certain cases, individuals may channel their sadness into creative outlets, such as writing, art, or music, as a form of expression and healing.

Recognizing how someone responds to sadness can inform approaches to supporting their well-being, whether through offering companionship, encouraging self-expression, or connecting them to resources.

Joy and Pro-Social or Reward-Seeking Behavior: Positive emotions, such as joy, happiness, and excitement, often lead to behaviors that reinforce social bonds, seek rewards, or savor positive experiences.

- **Social Connection:** Joy often prompts individuals to share their happiness with others, engage in celebrations, or strengthen social bonds through acts of kindness, generosity, or affection.

- **Exploration and Engagement:** Positive emotions can drive people to seek out new experiences, take on challenges, or engage in activities that bring further satisfaction and fulfillment.

- **Reinforcement of Habits:** When an action leads to a rewarding emotional response, such as joy or satisfaction, it becomes more likely that the person will repeat the behavior in the future. This principle underlies habits and learned behaviors.

By observing positive emotional responses, we can predict behaviors such as increased social engagement, risk-taking in pursuit of rewards, or commitment to activities that bring joy.

Emotional Responses and Decision-Making

Emotions significantly impact decision-making processes, often acting as "shortcuts" that guide choices quickly and efficiently. Emotional responses can override purely rational thinking, particularly in high-stress, high-stakes, or emotionally charged situations.

Fear-Based Decisions and Risk Aversion: Fear often leads individuals to make conservative or risk-averse decisions. For example, someone who fears failure may avoid taking on new challenges, even if the potential rewards are high. Similarly, fear of social rejection may prompt individuals to conform to group norms or avoid expressing unpopular opinions.

Anger and Impulsivity: Anger can lead to impulsive decision-making, as the emotional intensity may reduce a person's ability to consider the long-term consequences of their actions. People who are angry may make snap judgments, escalate conflicts, or make decisions aimed at seeking retribution. Recognizing this pattern can help de-escalate situations and guide individuals toward more thoughtful responses.

Optimism and Risk-Taking: Positive emotions, such as excitement and optimism, often lead to greater risk-taking and proactive decision-making. Optimistic individuals are more likely to pursue opportunities, try new things, and approach challenges with confidence. While this can lead to growth and innovation, it may also increase the risk of overlooking potential pitfalls.

Sadness and Cautious or Avoidant Decisions: Sadness can lead to more cautious or avoidant decision-making. People experiencing sadness may focus more on potential losses, weigh their decisions more carefully, or choose options that minimize risk. This state can slow decision-making processes but may also lead to more thorough and deliberate choices.

Emotional Triggers and Predictive Patterns

Emotional responses are often triggered by specific stimuli that are deeply rooted in individual experiences, beliefs, and values. Recognizing these triggers helps predict behavior and tailor responses that align with the person's emotional state.

Past Trauma and Avoidance Behavior: For individuals with past trauma, certain triggers may lead to avoidance behavior as a way to protect themselves from re-experiencing pain. For example, a person with a history of betrayal may avoid trusting others, even when trust is warranted. Recognizing this pattern helps anticipate avoidance behaviors and work toward building trust and safety.

Moral Beliefs and Advocacy or Confrontation: When people's deeply held moral beliefs are challenged, they may respond with strong emotions such as outrage or indignation. This often leads to behaviors such as advocacy, confrontation, or protest. Understanding these emotional responses helps predict how individuals will act when confronted with perceived injustice or ethical violations.

Contextual and Individual Differences in Predictive Behavior: While emotional responses offer valuable clues for predicting behavior, it is essential to consider individual differences and contextual factors that influence how emotions manifest.

Personality Traits and Emotion Regulation: Personality traits, such as conscientiousness, agreeableness, and neuroticism, shape how individuals regulate and respond to their emotions. For example, a highly conscientious person may channel anger into constructive problem-solving, while someone high in neuroticism may struggle to contain their emotional reactions.

Cultural and Social Influences: Cultural norms and social expectations shape how emotions are expressed and acted upon. In some cultures, expressing anger openly is discouraged, leading to more passive or indirect behaviors. Social influences, such as peer pressure or social norms, can also modify behavior based on emotional responses.

Situational Context: The specific context in which emotions are triggered also impacts behavior. For example, someone may react differently to criticism from a close friend than from a boss. Understanding the context helps predict whether behavior will be adaptive, defensive, or proactive.

Profiling Emotional Resilience and Vulnerability

Emotional resilience refers to an individual's ability to cope with stress, adversity, and change, bouncing back from difficult experiences with a sense of strength and growth. In contrast, emotional vulnerability describes the sensitivity or susceptibility to being emotionally affected by stressors, leading to greater difficulty in managing challenging emotions. While both resilience and vulnerability are shaped by a complex interplay of personality traits, life experiences, social support, and biological factors, profiling these characteristics can provide valuable insights into how individuals respond to life's challenges and the strategies they may need for growth and healing.

Emotional Resilience: Emotional resilience is the capacity to withstand and recover from stress, adversity, or setbacks. Resilient individuals tend to maintain a positive outlook, adapt to changing circumstances, and find constructive ways to cope with difficulties. Resilience does not mean an absence of negative emotions; rather, it is about navigating these emotions effectively and emerging stronger from challenging experiences.

Key Traits of Resilient Individuals:

- **Optimism:** Resilient people often maintain a hopeful and positive outlook, even in the face of hardship.

- **Adaptability:** They can adjust their thoughts, behaviors, and strategies to meet new challenges.

- **Emotional Regulation:** Resilient individuals are able to manage and control their emotions, preventing them from becoming overwhelming.

- **Problem-Solving Skills:** They approach challenges with a proactive mindset and are more likely to seek solutions rather than dwelling on problems.

- **Social Support Networks:** Strong relationships provide emotional support, validation, and practical assistance, bolstering resilience.

Emotional Vulnerability: Emotional vulnerability is characterized by heightened sensitivity to stress, criticism, or negative experiences. Vulnerable individuals may struggle to manage their emotions, experience intense reactions to stressors, and find it difficult to recover from setbacks. While vulnerability can make individuals more susceptible to negative outcomes, it also carries the potential for deeper empathy, connection, and emotional insight.

Key Traits of Vulnerable Individuals:

- **High Emotional Reactivity:** They may experience intense emotional responses to stressors or triggers.

- **Difficulty Coping with Stress:** Vulnerable individuals may struggle to manage stress or recover from emotional setbacks.

- **Sensitivity to Criticism and Rejection:** They are often more sensitive to perceived criticism, rejection, or failure.

- **Lower Perceived Control:** Vulnerable individuals may feel overwhelmed by challenges or believe that they have little control over their circumstances.

Emotional Resilience

Emotional resilience can be assessed and profiled based on a combination of personality traits, coping strategies, and environmental factors. Profiling resilience involves identifying the protective factors that help individuals withstand adversity and thrive despite difficult circumstances.

1. Personality Traits Associated with Resilience: Certain personality traits have been linked to greater resilience, making it easier for individuals to manage stress and adversity.

- **Conscientiousness:** Conscientious individuals tend to be organized, disciplined, and goal-oriented, which helps them maintain stability during challenging times.

- **Extraversion:** People high in extraversion often draw strength from social interactions, seeking support and building strong networks.

- **Openness to Experience:** Openness is linked to creativity and a willingness to adapt, which can help individuals navigate unfamiliar or stressful situations.

- **Emotional Stability (Low Neuroticism):** Individuals with lower levels of neuroticism are generally more emotionally stable and less prone to anxiety and negative emotional reactivity.

2. Coping Strategies and Resilience: Resilient individuals tend to use adaptive coping strategies to manage stress and adversity effectively.

- **Problem-Focused Coping:** Addressing the source of the stress through planning, problem-solving, or seeking solutions.

- **Emotional Regulation:** Using techniques such as mindfulness, relaxation, or reframing to manage intense emotions.

- **Social Support:** Building and maintaining supportive relationships that provide encouragement, validation, and practical help.

- **Growth Mindset:** Viewing setbacks as opportunities for growth and learning, rather than failures.

3. Environmental and Contextual Factors: Environmental factors, such as a supportive family, community resources, and access to healthcare, play a crucial role in fostering resilience. Resilient individuals often benefit from positive role models, nurturing relationships, and access to resources that promote well-being.

Emotional Vulnerability

Emotional vulnerability can be understood by examining the factors that increase sensitivity to stress, such as personality traits, past experiences, and coping mechanisms. Profiling vulnerability involves identifying areas where individuals may need additional support, as well as recognizing their unique strengths and sensitivities.

1. Personality Traits Associated with Vulnerability: Certain personality traits may contribute to heightened emotional vulnerability.

- **High Neuroticism:** Individuals high in neuroticism are more prone to experiencing negative emotions, such as anxiety, sadness, and irritability.

- **Low Self-Esteem:** Vulnerable individuals may struggle with feelings of inadequacy or worthlessness, making them more sensitive to criticism and rejection.

- **Introversion:** While introversion itself is not inherently negative, highly introverted individuals may experience greater vulnerability if they lack supportive social connections.

- **Perfectionism:** Striving for perfection can lead to feelings of failure, self-criticism, and heightened vulnerability to stress.

2. Coping Strategies and Vulnerability: Vulnerable individuals may rely on maladaptive coping strategies that can exacerbate stress and emotional difficulties.

- **Avoidance Coping:** Avoiding stressors or difficult emotions rather than confronting them can lead to unresolved issues and greater distress over time.

- **Rumination:** Repeatedly dwelling on negative thoughts or past experiences can intensify feelings of sadness, anxiety, or guilt.

- **Substance Use:** Some individuals may turn to alcohol, drugs, or other substances to cope with stress, which can worsen emotional vulnerability over time.

3. Past Experiences and Trauma: Traumatic or adverse life experiences often contribute to emotional vulnerability. Trauma survivors may be more sensitive to triggers and experience heightened emotional reactivity. Recognizing past trauma is crucial for profiling vulnerability and developing effective support strategies.

Chapter Seven: Lie Deception and Manipulation

Common Tactics

Manipulative people use various tactics to influence, control, or exploit others for their own benefit. Their behaviors often involve deceit, coercion, and emotional manipulation, aimed at undermining their target's confidence, decision-making, or autonomy. You must understand these tactics to recognize manipulation, set boundaries, and protect yourself from harm. Manipulative behaviors can occur in personal relationships, professional settings, and even larger social contexts.

Emotional Manipulation Tactics

Guilt-Tripping: Manipulative people often use guilt to control others by making them feel responsible for the manipulator's problems, emotions, or hardships. They may exaggerate their own suffering or frame themselves as the victim to induce feelings of guilt. Phrases such as, "After all I've done for you, this is how you treat me?" are common examples. The goal is to make the target feel indebted and compliant.

Gaslighting: Gaslighting involves manipulating someone into questioning their own reality, memory, or perceptions. A manipulator may deny events, distort facts, or accuse their target of being "too sensitive" or "crazy." Over time, this tactic can erode the target's confidence and sense of reality, making them more dependent on the manipulator for validation and guidance.

Love-Bombing: This tactic involves overwhelming someone with excessive attention, affection, and praise early in a relationship to gain their trust and loyalty. Once the target becomes emotionally invested, the manipulator may withdraw their affection, use it as leverage, or switch to more controlling behaviors. Love-bombing is common in abusive relationships, as it creates a strong emotional bond that makes it difficult for the target to leave.

Emotional Blackmail: Manipulative individuals may use threats, ultimatums, or appeals to fear to control someone's actions. For example, they may say, "If you leave me, I'll hurt myself" or "If you don't do what I want, you'll ruin everything." This tactic exploits the target's empathy, fear, or obligation to coerce compliance.

Control and Domination Tactics

Isolation: Manipulative people often seek to isolate their target from friends, family, or support networks to make them more dependent on the manipulator. This may involve sowing distrust, creating conflict with others, or controlling the target's time and interactions. Isolation reduces the target's ability to seek alternative perspectives or support.

Withholding Information: By selectively providing or concealing information, a manipulative person can maintain power and control over a situation. This tactic often leaves the target feeling uncertain, confused, or unable to make informed decisions. Manipulators may "forget" to mention important details or deliberately obscure their intentions.

Triangulation: Triangulation occurs when a manipulative person uses a third party to create conflict, jealousy, or rivalry, often to maintain control or shift blame. For example, they may involve another person in a dispute to divide and conquer, making themselves appear superior or indispensable. This tactic keeps the target off balance and undermines their relationships with others.

Silent Treatment: The silent treatment involves withdrawing communication or affection as a means of punishment and control. By refusing to engage, the manipulator puts the target in a state of uncertainty, forcing them to apologize, comply, or seek reconciliation. This tactic plays on the target's fear of abandonment or rejection.

Deception and Manipulative Communication

Lying and Exaggeration: Manipulative people may lie outright or exaggerate facts to gain the upper hand. This can include distorting past events, fabricating stories, or making empty promises. By controlling the narrative, manipulators can influence others' perceptions and keep themselves in a position of power.

Blame Shifting and Projection: When confronted, manipulative individuals often deflect responsibility by blaming others or projecting their own behavior onto their target. For example, a manipulator accused of dishonesty might accuse their partner of being untrustworthy. This tactic creates confusion and shifts focus away from their own behavior.

Playing the Victim: Manipulative people may feign helplessness, sadness, or victimhood to gain sympathy, attention, or special treatment. By portraying themselves as the victim, they can deflect criticism, elicit pity, and make others feel responsible for their well-being. This tactic often makes it difficult for the target to set boundaries or hold the manipulator accountable.

Using Flattery and Charm: Manipulators often use flattery, compliments, and charm to lower their target's defenses and gain trust. They may appear genuine, likable, and persuasive, making it harder for their targets to recognize their true motives. Once trust is established, they may begin to exploit or manipulate their target.

Vague or Ambiguous Communication: Manipulative people may deliberately use vague language, contradictions, or ambiguous statements to create confusion and maintain control. When confronted, they may deny having said certain things, reinterpret their words, or claim to be misunderstood, leaving their target unsure of what was agreed upon or discussed.

Coercive and Aggressive Tactics

Intimidation and Threats: Manipulators may use intimidation or veiled threats to force compliance. This can involve verbal abuse, physical posturing, or implicit threats, such as suggesting negative consequences if their demands are not met. This tactic plays on fear and can quickly escalate into more abusive behaviors.

Constant Criticism and Demeaning Remarks: Manipulative individuals may undermine their target's confidence and self-esteem through constant criticism, belittling comments, or put-downs. By making their target feel inadequate or unworthy, they can maintain control and make it difficult for the target to stand up for themselves.

Denial and Minimization: When confronted with their actions, manipulative people may deny any wrongdoing or minimize the impact of their behavior. They might say, "You're overreacting," or "It wasn't a big deal," to invalidate the target's feelings and make them question their own perceptions. This tactic shifts responsibility away from the manipulator and onto the target.

Manipulating Boundaries and Expectations

Boundary Testing and Overstepping: Manipulators often test boundaries by pushing limits, breaking rules, or making unreasonable demands. If the target does not enforce their boundaries, the manipulator will continue to overstep, often escalating their demands over time. This tactic establishes a power imbalance and makes it difficult for the target to assert their own needs.

Feigning Confusion or Incompetence: In some cases, manipulators may pretend not to understand requests, act incompetent, or feign helplessness to avoid responsibility or make their target do more work. This tactic shifts the burden onto the target and keeps the manipulator in control of the situation.

Overpromising and Underdelivering: Manipulative people may make grand promises or commitments to gain trust or cooperation, only to fail to follow through. By dangling the prospect of future rewards or changes, they keep their target hopeful and engaged, even when the promises are unlikely to be fulfilled.

Spotting Inconsistencies and Half-Truths

Spotting inconsistencies and half-truths is a valuable skill for evaluating the honesty and reliability of information, whether in personal relationships, professional settings, or public discourse. Inconsistencies occur when there are contradictions or changes in a person's statements, behavior, or actions, while half-truths involve statements that are partially true but intentionally omit key details or distort the overall context.

Recognizing Inconsistencies in Communication

Inconsistent communication often signals that something is amiss, whether it is the result of intentional deception, a lapse in memory, or stress. The key to spotting inconsistencies lies in paying close attention to both what is said and how it is delivered.

Contradictory Statements: A common sign of inconsistency is when a person's statements conflict with one another over time. For example, if someone provides different versions of the same event or changes key details, it may indicate that they are being dishonest or trying to hide something. In casual conversation, this might sound like, "Yesterday, I worked late until 9 PM," and later, "I was at the gym around 8 PM."

Shifts in Story Details: When a person's story changes—whether in small details or major points—it can raise red flags. While minor shifts may sometimes be attributed to memory lapses, significant changes without a reasonable explanation suggest a potential attempt to cover up inconsistencies or mislead others. An example of this might be a coworker who initially says, "I spoke to the client this morning," but later claims, "I emailed the client yesterday."

Conflicting Non-Verbal Cues: Inconsistent body language, facial expressions, or tone of voice can reveal incongruence between what someone is saying and how they are feeling. For example, a person may say, "I'm fine" while displaying a tense posture, avoiding eye contact, or exhibiting a forced smile. Non-verbal cues often betray true emotions, making them a useful tool for identifying inconsistencies.

Evasive or Vague Answers: People who provide inconsistent or evasive answers may try to avoid direct questions or change the subject. If someone becomes vague, offers non-answers, or frequently redirects conversations, it can signal that they are uncomfortable or hiding something. For example, when asked about their involvement in a project, they might reply with, "Oh, that was a while ago" or "It doesn't really matter," instead of providing a clear response.

Identifying Half-Truths and Misleading Information

Half-truths are statements that contain elements of truth but are incomplete or misleading. This type of communication is often used to create a specific impression while omitting key information that would change the perception of the statement.

Selective Disclosure: A half-truth often involves sharing selective information that supports the desired narrative while omitting details that contradict it. For example, someone might say, "I've always been honest with you about where I was," but fail to mention critical details about who they were with or why they were there. This selective approach gives the impression of full transparency while concealing important facts.

Context Manipulation: Half-truths may involve presenting facts in a misleading context. For example, a salesperson might say, "This product has the highest safety rating" without disclosing that the rating was based on outdated criteria or compared to a limited set of competitors. This tactic relies on technically accurate information presented in a way that distorts the true picture.

Minimization or Exaggeration: A person using half-truths may minimize negative information or exaggerate positive details to manipulate perceptions. For example, someone discussing their role in a project might emphasize their contributions while downplaying their mistakes or failures. Statements such as, "I played a key role in making this happen" may be true, but the omission of significant challenges or setbacks can mislead others about the full story.

Avoidance of Direct Answers: Half-truths often involve providing partial responses to direct questions. For example, if asked, "Did you finish the report?" a person might reply, "I've been working on it," which suggests progress but avoids confirming whether the task is complete. This tactic creates an impression of transparency while withholding important details.

Spotting Inconsistencies and Half-Truths

To effectively spot inconsistencies and half-truths, consider using the following strategies:

1. Ask Clarifying Questions: One of the best ways to identify inconsistencies or half-truths is to ask direct and clarifying questions. For example, if a person's story changes or seems incomplete, ask them to explain specific details or elaborate on their earlier statements. Be polite but firm, and watch for signs of evasion, discomfort, or further shifts in their account.

2. Listen for Repetition and Over-Explanation: People who are trying to maintain a deceptive narrative may repeat key points or offer excessive details in an attempt to appear credible. Over-explaining or providing information that was not requested can be a red flag, as it may indicate an effort to control the conversation and create a specific impression.

3. Observe Body Language and Non-Verbal Cues: Body language often reveals inconsistencies that words alone may not convey. Watch for signs of nervousness, such as fidgeting, avoiding eye contact, or changes in tone and pace of speech. If non-verbal cues conflict with verbal statements, it may indicate discomfort or dishonesty.

4. Cross-Check Information: If possible, verify the accuracy of what someone is saying by cross-checking their statements with other sources or evidence. This could involve speaking with other individuals, reviewing documents, or comparing previous accounts. Inconsistencies between different sources of information can reveal gaps or distortions in the narrative.

5. Consider the Context and Motivation: People often tailor their communication to serve a particular purpose or protect themselves from negative outcomes. Consider what motivations the individual might have for providing incomplete or misleading information. This context can help you understand why they might be withholding or distorting the truth.

6. Be Patient and Observant: Manipulative people often rely on confusion, quick changes, or emotional pressure to maintain control. By remaining patient, listening carefully, and giving the person space to elaborate on their statements, you can create opportunities for inconsistencies or half-truths to become apparent.

Practical Examples of Spotting Inconsistencies and Half-Truths

In the Workplace: A colleague claims to have completed a task but cannot provide details about how or when it was finished. When asked, their response shifts, and they provide vague or contradictory explanations.

In Personal Relationships: A friend mentions being busy on a certain day but later shares a social media post suggesting they were elsewhere. When confronted, they give a partial explanation that minimizes their initial statement without fully addressing the discrepancy.

In Public Communication: A public figure or spokesperson may provide selective statistics to support a policy while omitting context or relevant data that would cast doubt on their claims. By examining the broader context and cross-referencing sources, half-truths become easier to identify.

Profiling Pathological Liars and Manipulators

Pathological liars and manipulators are individuals who engage in habitual deceit, often using lies and manipulation as a primary means of interaction. While everyone may lie occasionally, pathological liars compulsively and frequently lie, even when it serves no clear purpose. Manipulators, on the other hand, intentionally influence, control, or exploit others through deceit, coercion, or emotional manipulation.

Pathological Liars

Pathological lying, also known as "pseudologia fantastica" or "mythomania," involves a chronic tendency to lie compulsively. Unlike occasional lies told to avoid embarrassment or protect someone's feelings, pathological lies are often disproportionate, elaborate, and sometimes entirely baseless. The behavior is deeply ingrained and may be difficult to change.

Characteristics of Pathological Liars:

- **Compulsive Lying:** Pathological liars lie habitually and compulsively, even when there is no obvious benefit. They may lie about small, inconsequential matters or invent elaborate stories to gain attention or sympathy.

- **Lack of Apparent Motive:** Unlike lies told for specific gain or protection, pathological lies often appear purposeless, serving no clear advantage to the liar. This behavior can be confusing and perplexing to those around them.

- **Inconsistent Narratives:** Pathological liars frequently change their stories or add new, contradictory details over time. When challenged, they may continue to lie or shift their account to maintain control of the narrative.

- **Superficial Charm:** Many pathological liars are skilled at making a positive impression. They may appear charismatic, confident, and convincing, which can make their lies difficult to detect, especially during first impressions.

- **Difficulty Admitting the Truth:** Even when confronted with clear evidence, pathological liars may double down on their falsehoods or deny wrongdoing. Admitting the truth is often seen as a threat to their self-image or control.

Potential Underlying Factors: The causes of pathological lying are complex and may include personality disorders (such as narcissistic personality disorder or antisocial personality disorder), unresolved trauma, low self-esteem, or a desire to maintain a false image. In some cases, the behavior may be linked to neurological or psychological conditions, though not all pathological liars have diagnosable disorders.

Characteristics and Tactics of Manipulators

Manipulators use deceit, coercion, and subtle control tactics to influence others for their own gain. While not all manipulators are pathological liars, many use lies as part of their manipulation strategy. They often exhibit a pattern of behavior designed to undermine, control, or exploit their targets.

Key Traits of Manipulators:

- **High Emotional Intelligence (Used Unethically):** Many manipulators have a keen sense of other people's emotions, needs, and weaknesses. They use this knowledge to influence, exploit, or control others, often appearing empathetic or charming initially.

- **Lack of Empathy:** Manipulators are often unable or unwilling to consider the impact of their actions on others. They may rationalize their behavior, justify harm, or show little remorse for their actions.

- **Desire for Control and Power:** Manipulators seek to dominate or control their relationships, workplaces, or social interactions. They may use subtle or overt means to achieve this, from emotional blackmail to overt intimidation.

- **Self-Centeredness:** Manipulators often prioritize their own desires, goals, or feelings above all else. Their actions frequently center around fulfilling their needs at the expense of others.

Profiling Pathological Liars and Manipulators in Context

1. In Personal Relationships: Pathological liars and manipulators in personal relationships often create a cycle of emotional highs and lows. They may shower their partners or friends with affection, only to lie, deceive, or manipulate them later. The inconsistency in their behavior can lead to confusion, self-doubt, and dependency on the manipulator for validation or clarity. Key signs include repeated lies, gaslighting, shifting blame, and a tendency to control the narrative.

2. In Professional Settings: In workplaces, pathological liars and manipulators may engage in behaviors such as exaggerating their achievements, taking credit for others' work, undermining colleagues, or spreading misinformation. They often seek to advance their own agenda by manipulating workplace dynamics, creating alliances, and playing on power dynamics. Their behavior may lead to a toxic work environment, with colleagues feeling distrustful or manipulated.

3. In Social and Public Roles: Manipulators in public roles may use charisma, charm, and persuasive speech to influence groups, maintain a favorable image, or exploit others for personal gain. Their ability to twist facts, present half-truths, and deflect criticism can make them difficult to challenge or expose.

Responses and Protection Against Manipulation

Responding to and protecting oneself against manipulation requires a thoughtful, ethical approach that preserves personal integrity, fosters healthy boundaries, and promotes accountability.

Principles for Responding to Manipulation

Responding to manipulation ethically means maintaining your values, acting with integrity, and avoiding behaviors that perpetuate harm or escalation. Here are key ethical principles to consider:

1. Respect for Autonomy: An ethical response respects both your autonomy and the autonomy of the manipulative person. This involves asserting your boundaries and making decisions based on your own needs and values, while also recognizing that the manipulator is responsible for their own behavior.

- **Example:** When faced with emotional blackmail, such as "If you leave, I'll be devastated," respond by acknowledging their feelings but reaffirming your right to make choices. You might say, "I understand this is difficult for you, but I need to make this decision for myself."

2. Honesty and Directness: Being truthful and direct is essential when addressing manipulative behavior. Ethical responses avoid deceit, passive-aggression, or retaliation. Instead, aim to communicate openly and clearly.

- **Example:** If someone is using guilt to manipulate you, you can respond by saying, "I understand you're upset, but I feel uncomfortable when guilt is used to influence my decisions. Let's discuss this openly."

3. Empathy with Boundaries: While it is important to be empathetic, this empathy should not come at the cost of your well-being or boundaries. Acknowledge the manipulator's feelings without letting them override your own needs or values.

- **Example:** "I hear that you're feeling hurt. I care about your feelings, but I also need to prioritize my own needs."

4. Non-Escalation and Calmness: Manipulative people often try to provoke strong emotional reactions. Maintaining calm and composed communication helps prevent escalation and ensures that you stay in control of your response.

- **Example:** If someone tries to provoke anger through insults or accusations, respond with calm detachment: "I'd like to continue this conversation respectfully. If that's not possible, we can take a break and revisit it later."

Strategies for Protecting Against Manipulation

Ethical responses to manipulation go hand in hand with proactive strategies for protecting yourself. These strategies help maintain your emotional well-being and assertiveness in the face of manipulative behaviors.

1. Establish and Communicate Boundaries: Setting clear boundaries is essential for preventing manipulation. Clearly communicate what behaviors you will and will not tolerate, and be prepared to enforce these boundaries if necessary.

- **Example:** "I'm happy to discuss this issue, but I will not engage if you continue to raise your voice or use insults."

2. Practice Assertive Communication: Assertive communication involves expressing your thoughts, feelings, and needs openly and respectfully. It is different from passive, aggressive, or passive-aggressive communication and can help deter manipulative behavior.

- **Example:** "I feel uncomfortable when you pressure me to agree quickly. I need more time to think this over."

3. Be Mindful of Emotional Triggers: Manipulators often target emotional vulnerabilities. Becoming aware of your emotional triggers helps you recognize when someone is attempting to manipulate you and respond thoughtfully rather than react impulsively.

- **Example:** If guilt is a common trigger, practice recognizing guilt-inducing statements and reframing your internal response. Remind yourself that setting boundaries is not selfish.

4. Seek Clarity and Verification: Manipulative people often use ambiguous statements or withhold information. Asking clarifying questions and seeking verification helps counter their tactics and brings transparency to the situation.

- **Example:** "Can you provide specific examples of what you're referring to?" or "I'd like to confirm the details with other sources before making a decision."

5. Document Interactions When Necessary: In professional settings or in cases of ongoing manipulation, keeping a record of interactions can provide clarity and protect against misrepresentation or deceit. Documentation may be useful for reference or for escalating concerns if necessary.

6. Limit or Disengage When Appropriate: In some cases, disengaging from a manipulative relationship or situation may be the most ethical and self-protective course of action. This can involve reducing contact, seeking a neutral third party, or ending the relationship altogether.

- **Example:** "I value our relationship, but I need space to reflect. We can revisit this when we are both ready for an honest and respectful conversation."

Chapter Eight: Profiling Through Social Media and Digital Behavior

Viral trends—such as challenges, memes, or hashtags—spread rapidly across social media platforms, often capturing widespread attention within a short period. These trends may involve humor, dance, social causes, or challenges that encourage user participation and sharing.

Implications:

- **Collective Participation:** Viral trends can foster a sense of community and belonging as people join in and share their own contributions.

- **Influence on Behavior:** Trends can encourage positive behaviors (e.g., fundraising challenges) or potentially risky or harmful behaviors (e.g., dangerous stunts).

- **Marketing and Branding Opportunities:** Companies often capitalize on viral trends to boost engagement, create brand awareness, or promote products.

- **Short-Term Attention Span:** The rapid pace of social media trends can contribute to short-lived engagement, with attention quickly shifting from one trend to another.

2. Curated Self-Presentation: Social media often encourages users to curate their online personas, selectively sharing highlights of their lives while omitting less flattering or mundane aspects. This "highlight reel" approach can create an idealized and sometimes unrealistic portrayal of life.

Implications:

- **Impact on Self-Esteem and Comparison:** Constant exposure to curated, seemingly perfect content can lead to social comparison, lower self-esteem, and feelings of inadequacy, particularly among young users.

- **Authenticity vs. Performance:** The desire to appear impressive or relatable may lead to performative behavior, making it difficult to distinguish genuine expression from staged content.

- **Social Influence:** Influencers and public figures who curate their image can shape trends, values, and behaviors among their followers.

3. Echo Chambers and Filter Bubbles: Social media algorithms often prioritize content that aligns with users' existing beliefs, interests, and preferences. This can create echo chambers—environments where users are primarily exposed to information that reinforces their views—and filter bubbles, where diverse perspectives are limited.

Implications:

- **Polarization of Opinions:** Echo chambers can contribute to increased polarization, as users are rarely exposed to dissenting viewpoints or nuanced debates.

- **Confirmation Bias:** The constant reinforcement of existing beliefs can strengthen biases and hinder critical thinking.

- **Challenges to Democratic Discourse:** Filter bubbles may reduce exposure to balanced information, posing challenges to informed decision-making in democratic processes.

4. **Misinformation and Disinformation**: Misinformation (false or misleading information) and disinformation (deliberately deceptive content) spread quickly on social media due to the viral nature of posts, lack of content verification, and algorithmic amplification.

Implications:

- **Public Mistrust:** The prevalence of misinformation can erode public trust in institutions, media, and science.

- **Real-World Consequences:** Misinformation campaigns have been linked to political unrest, public health crises, and harmful behaviors (e.g., vaccine hesitancy).

- **Fact-Checking Efforts:** Social media platforms have introduced fact-checking measures, but these efforts face challenges in implementation and effectiveness.

5. Influencer Culture and Micro-Influencing: The rise of influencers—individuals with large followings who promote products, lifestyles, or ideas—has transformed social media into a powerful tool for marketing and social influence. Even micro-influencers, who have smaller but highly engaged audiences, play a role in shaping consumer behavior and trends.

Implications:

- **Commercialization of Personal Lives:** Influencers often monetize their lives, blurring the lines between genuine content and sponsored advertising.

- **Cultural Trends and Values:** Influencers can shape beauty standards, lifestyle choices, and social norms, often with global reach.

- **Consumer Skepticism:** The commercialization of content may lead to skepticism and distrust among users, particularly when influencers lack transparency about sponsored content.

6. Hashtag Activism and Social Movements: Social media has become a platform for activism, with hashtags and viral campaigns mobilizing support for social, political, and humanitarian causes. Examples include movements like #MeToo, #BlackLivesMatter, and climate change advocacy.

Implications:

- **Amplification of Voices:** Social media provides a platform for marginalized voices and allows issues to gain visibility and support on a global scale.

- **Rapid Mobilization:** Hashtag activism enables the rapid dissemination of information, petitions, protests, and fundraising efforts.

- **Challenges of Slacktivism:** Critics argue that social media activism can sometimes be superficial or performative, with users engaging in "clicktivism" without meaningful follow-through.

Psychological and Social Impacts of Social Media Content Patterns

1. Mental Health and Well-Being: The constant exposure to curated content, social comparison, and online interactions can impact mental health in both positive and negative ways.

- **Positive Impacts:** Social media can provide support networks, foster a sense of belonging, and offer educational and inspirational content.

- **Negative Impacts:** Excessive use, cyberbullying, and comparison with idealized portrayals can contribute to anxiety, depression, and feelings of isolation.

2. Social Validation and Dopamine Feedback Loops: Social media platforms often rely on likes, shares, and comments to engage users, creating a dopamine-driven feedback loop that reinforces behavior.

- **Addictive Behavior:** The pursuit of social validation can lead to compulsive use and overreliance on external affirmation.

- **Pressure to Perform:** Users may feel pressured to create content that garners attention, likes, or approval, leading to stress and anxiety.

3. Shaping Perceptions and Public Opinion: Social media patterns influence how people perceive themselves, others, and global issues.

- **Agenda Setting:** Viral posts and popular accounts can shape public discourse, determining which issues receive attention and how they are framed.

- **Stereotyping and Bias Reinforcement:** Repeated exposure to certain types of content can reinforce stereotypes, stigmas, or biases, affecting how people view specific groups or issues.

Navigating Social Media Content Patterns Ethically

1. Critical Consumption and Media Literacy: Encouraging critical thinking and media literacy helps users evaluate the credibility of content, identify biases, and resist manipulation.

- **Fact-Checking and Verification:** Users should verify information from multiple credible sources before sharing or acting on it.

- **Understanding Algorithms:** Awareness of how algorithms prioritize content can help users break out of echo chambers and seek diverse perspectives.

2. Promoting Authenticity and Transparency: Influencers, content creators, and everyday users can promote authenticity by sharing real, unfiltered moments and being transparent about sponsored content or motives.

3. Supporting Positive Trends and Movements: Engaging in hashtag activism, supporting positive social campaigns, and amplifying marginalized voices can leverage social media's power for good.

4. Setting Healthy Boundaries: Balancing online and offline interactions, setting limits on screen time, and focusing on meaningful connections can mitigate the negative effects of social media.

Digital Footprints: What Posts, Likes, and Shares Say About a Person

In today's interconnected digital world, everything we post, like, and share on social media leaves a trail—our digital footprint. This collection of online actions provides a snapshot of our interests, beliefs, values, and even aspects of our personality.

A digital footprint consists of the information and traces a person leaves behind when they use the internet. This footprint can be both active (content we intentionally create, such as posts, photos, and comments) and passive (information collected about us without our explicit input, such as browsing history or location data). Our online behavior—what we choose to share, interact with, and amplify—shapes our digital presence and how others perceive us.

Key Components of a Digital Footprint:

- **Posts and Comments:** Publicly shared thoughts, opinions, photos, and videos that reflect an individual's interests, beliefs, and lifestyle.

- **Likes, Shares, and Reactions:** Engagements with others' content that reveal preferences, values, and social affiliations.

- **Search and Browsing History:** Data collected by search engines and websites that indicate areas of interest, research, or curiosity.

What Posts Say About a Person

The content a person posts on social media platforms often reveals aspects of their identity, values, and motivations. Posts can serve as expressions of creativity, tools for connection, or ways to engage in social and political discourse.

1. Personal Interests and Passions: Posts that focus on hobbies, travel experiences, or creative projects provide insight into a person's interests and what brings them joy. For example, someone who frequently shares photos of hiking trips likely enjoys nature and outdoor adventures.

2. Beliefs and Values: People often use social media as a platform to express their beliefs and values, whether through advocacy posts, participation in social movements, or commentary on current events. Posts that align with causes like environmental conservation, social justice, or political issues reflect the priorities and principles that shape an individual's worldview.

3. Emotional State and Personality: Posts can also provide a window into a person's emotional state or personality. Consistently positive, humorous, or motivational posts may reflect an optimistic outlook or a desire to uplift others, while posts expressing frustration, sadness, or vulnerability may indicate a willingness to share more personal aspects of life.

4. Professional and Personal Branding: Social media platforms like LinkedIn or Twitter are often used to build professional identities and networks. Posts that highlight career achievements, share industry insights, or engage in relevant conversations shape a person's professional image and aspirations.

Implications:

- **Public Perception and Reputation:** Posts contribute to how others perceive a person, both positively and negatively. For example, inappropriate or offensive posts can damage one's reputation, while thoughtful contributions can enhance credibility.

- **Employer Scrutiny:** Employers frequently review candidates' social media profiles during hiring processes. Posts reflecting professionalism, integrity, and alignment with company values can be advantageous, while controversial or inappropriate content may raise concerns.

What Likes and Shares Reveal

Engagement with social media content—through likes, shares, reactions, and comments—provides additional insight into a person's values, preferences, and social affiliations. These interactions often reflect what a person finds interesting, entertaining, or worthy of amplification.

1. Preferences and Interests: Likes and shares reveal a person's taste in music, books, movies, or social causes. Repeated engagement with specific types of content signals an interest in those topics. For example, a user who consistently likes posts about new tech gadgets likely has a passion for technology.

2. Social and Political Leanings: Liking or sharing posts that align with specific political views or social issues indicates where a person stands on key issues. This engagement can shape public conversations and demonstrate solidarity with particular movements or ideologies.

3. Social Affiliations and Peer Influence: People are often influenced by the content shared within their social circles. Liking or sharing friends' posts can reflect social norms, relationship dynamics, or a desire to maintain connections. Peer influence may drive engagement with trending topics, viral challenges, or community causes.

4. Personality Traits and Behavior Patterns: Studies suggest that patterns of likes and shares can reveal personality traits such as openness, extraversion, or agreeableness. For instance, people who frequently like and share content on social causes may score higher on measures of empathy and social responsibility.

Implications:

- **Algorithmic Influence:** Social media algorithms use engagement data to personalize content feeds, potentially reinforcing echo chambers or biases by showing more of what a person already likes.

- **Privacy Concerns:** Likes and shares can expose sensitive information, even when not explicitly stated. For example, engaging with certain health-related content may inadvertently reveal medical conditions or interests.

The Broader Implications of Digital Footprints

1. **Data Collection and Profiling**: Social media platforms and advertisers use data from posts, likes, and shares to create detailed profiles of users. This data drives targeted advertising, content recommendations, and sometimes manipulative practices, such as influencing political views through tailored content.

2. **Social Influence and Echo Chambers**: Engagement patterns shape social influence and reinforce echo chambers, where users are primarily exposed to content that aligns with their existing beliefs. This can limit exposure to diverse perspectives and deepen ideological divides.

3. **Ethical Considerations in Self-Presentation**: The desire to maintain a positive digital footprint can lead to

curated, idealized self-presentation. This practice raises ethical considerations about authenticity, self-worth, and the impact of social comparison on mental health.

4. Digital Legacy and Long-Term Impact: A person's digital footprint can have long-term implications. Content shared online may resurface years later, impacting personal and professional opportunities. This underscores the importance of mindful posting and engagement.

Tips for Managing and Shaping Your Digital Footprint

1. Think Before You Post: Consider the potential impact of your posts on your reputation, relationships, and career. Ask yourself whether the content aligns with your values and how it might be perceived by others.

2. Review and Curate Your Content: Periodically review your social media profiles and delete or archive posts that no longer reflect who you are or that could be misinterpreted.

3. Engage Mindfully: Be selective about what you like, share, and comment on. Recognize that these interactions contribute to your digital footprint and influence what content is promoted in your network.

4. Protect Your Privacy: Use privacy settings to control who can see your posts and interactions. Be cautious about sharing personal information that could be used for malicious purposes.

5. Be Transparent and Authentic: When appropriate, be authentic in your online presence, sharing a balanced view of your experiences and beliefs. This can help build genuine connections and credibility.

Profiling Online Behavior in Professional and Personal Contexts

In a professional context, online behavior typically revolves around maintaining a positive image, building a personal brand, networking, and demonstrating expertise. Platforms like LinkedIn, industry forums, and professional blogs are common spaces for showcasing one's skills, experience, and thought leadership.

Key Elements of Professional Online Behavior:

- **Professional Branding and Content Creation:** Many professionals use social media to build a personal brand by sharing industry insights, thought leadership articles, or commentary on relevant topics. These posts often reflect their expertise, interests, and career goals.

- **Networking and Engagement:** Professionals often engage with industry peers through comments, discussions, and endorsements. Networking online can lead to new job opportunities, partnerships, or collaborations.

- **Professionalism and Respectful Communication:** Maintaining a respectful, courteous tone is crucial in professional interactions.

Disrespectful or inflammatory comments can damage a person's reputation and career prospects.

- **Transparency and Authenticity:** While professionalism is key, many professionals strike a balance by showing aspects of their personality, hobbies, or values to appear relatable and human.

Implications of Professional Online Behavior:

- **Reputation and Employability:** Employers often review candidates' online profiles as part of the hiring process. A strong, positive online presence can enhance employability, while inappropriate content, unprofessional language, or controversial opinions may raise red flags.

- **Networking and Influence:** Online behavior can impact professional influence and credibility. Sharing insightful content, engaging in meaningful discussions, and building a positive reputation can strengthen one's professional network.

- **Potential Pitfalls:** Unprofessional conduct, oversharing, or engaging in online conflicts can harm one's professional standing. Even posts made in personal settings may have professional consequences if they are publicly visible or go viral.

Tips for Profiling Professional Online Behavior:

- **Analyze Content Quality:** Evaluate the relevance, accuracy, and tone of shared content. Does it align with the individual's stated expertise and professional goals?

- **Observe Engagement Patterns:** How often does the individual interact with peers or industry leaders? Do their engagements reflect genuine interest, support, or thought leadership?

- **Review Consistency:** Is there a consistent, cohesive image across different platforms, or do their interactions reveal conflicting personas?

Personal Online Behavior

In a personal context, online behavior reflects an individual's identity, interests, values, and social interactions. Social media platforms like Facebook, Instagram, Twitter, and TikTok often serve as outlets for self-expression, social connection, and entertainment.

Key Elements of Personal Online Behavior:

- **Self-Expression and Identity:** People use social media to share their thoughts, experiences, interests, and creative pursuits. This content often reveals aspects of their personality, values, and lifestyle.

- **Social Interaction and Relationship Building:** Online behavior in personal contexts includes connecting with friends, family, and communities. Posts, likes, comments, and messages reflect social ties and relationship dynamics.

- **Engagement with Content:** What a person likes, shares, or comments on offers clues about their preferences, humor, political views, and more. These engagements contribute to shaping their digital footprint.

- **Privacy and Boundaries:** Some individuals carefully manage their online presence, limiting what they share and controlling their audience. Others may be more open, sharing personal milestones, thoughts, or opinions freely.

Implications of Personal Online Behavior:

- **Social Perception and Relationships:** Online behavior shapes how others perceive us, influencing friendships, romantic relationships, and even broader social interactions.

- **Privacy Risks:** Sharing personal information, location data, or private thoughts can expose individuals to privacy risks, online harassment, or identity theft.

- **Potential Overlap with Professional Life:** Even posts made in a personal capacity can affect one's professional reputation if they become widely circulated or viewed by colleagues, employers, or clients.

Tips for Profiling Personal Online Behavior:

- **Assess Content Diversity:** What topics does the individual frequently post about? Is their content focused on personal milestones, hobbies, political opinions, or humor?

- **Observe Social Connections:** How does the individual interact with their social circle? Do they exhibit supportive, confrontational, or passive behaviors?

- **Consider Privacy Settings:** Is the person's online presence public or restricted to certain audiences? This reflects their comfort with public visibility and how they manage boundaries.

Overlapping and Distinguishing Professional and Personal Behavior

The line between professional and personal online behavior can be thin. While some people maintain strict boundaries, others allow aspects of their personal lives to blend into their professional personas. Understanding when and how these behaviors intersect is key to accurately profiling someone's online presence.

Potential Overlaps:

- **Personal Values and Professional Advocacy:** Professionals may share personal posts advocating for social, environmental, or political causes that align with their values. This can reflect a commitment to certain beliefs but may also impact how they are perceived professionally.

- **Blended Content Creation:** Influencers, entrepreneurs, and public figures often blend personal stories and professional expertise to create a relatable online presence.

- **Networking and Personal Connections:** Engaging with professional peers in informal settings can build rapport and deepen connections but may also require mindful communication.

Key Considerations for Managing Overlapping Behavior:

- **Mindfulness and Consistency:** Being consistent in values and tone across platforms helps create a cohesive digital identity while minimizing risks of contradictory behavior.

- **Boundary Setting:** Clearly defining and maintaining boundaries, such as using different platforms for personal and professional interactions, can help individuals manage their online presence effectively.

- **Ethical Responsibility:** Professionals must be aware of how their personal posts could impact their employer, colleagues, or clients. Ethical conduct is key to building and maintaining trust.

Recommended Resources

Profiling, as a field of study, spans diverse disciplines, including psychology, criminology, sociology, behavioral analysis, and interpersonal communication. Whether you are interested in understanding human behavior, criminal profiling, or applying profiling skills in professional settings, deepening your knowledge requires exploring a range of resources that offer theoretical frameworks, practical techniques, and case studies. Here is a curated list of recommended materials for further study in profiling, categorized by books, multimedia resources, and specific areas of focus.

Foundational Books

- *The Gift of Fear: Survival Signals That Protect Us from Violence* by Gavin de Becker. This book offers practical insights into human behavior, intuition, and how to recognize warning signs that can help prevent violence and stay safe.

- *Mindhunter: Inside the FBI's Elite Serial Crime Unit* by John E. Douglas and Mark Olshaker. A fascinating exploration of criminal profiling by one of the pioneers in the field, providing real-life case studies and insights into the minds of violent criminals.

- *Criminal Profiling: An Introduction to Behavioral Evidence Analysis* by Brent E. Turvey. A comprehensive resource that delves into criminal profiling techniques, ethical considerations, and real-world applications of profiling in criminal investigations.

Psychological and Personality Profiling:

- *The Psychopath Test: A Journey Through the Madness Industry* by Jon Ronson A gripping exploration of psychopathy, the diagnostic process, and the complexities of identifying and profiling individuals with psychopathic traits.

- *Personality Types: Using the Enneagram for Self-Discovery* by Don Richard Riso and Russ Hudson. This book provides a detailed look at the Enneagram personality system, offering insights into motivations, behavior patterns, and interpersonal dynamics.

- *The Big Five Personality Traits* (various scholarly articles and texts) Studying the Big Five model of personality (Openness, Conscientiousness, Extraversion, Agreeableness, Neuroticism) helps understand how these traits shape behavior and interactions.

Body Language and Nonverbal Communication:

- *What Every BODY is Saying: An Ex-FBI Agent's Guide to Speed-Reading People* by Joe Navarro. Navarro, a former FBI counterintelligence officer, explains how to interpret nonverbal cues and body language to gain insights into a person's emotions, intentions, and behavior.

- *The Definitive Book of Body Language* by Allan and
  Barbara   Pease
  A practical guide to understanding and interpreting
  nonverbal communication cues, from facial expressions
  to gestures.

Multimedia and Interactive Resources

Podcasts:

- *Criminal.* This true-crime podcast delves into various
  aspects of criminal behavior, including psychological
  profiles of offenders and investigative techniques.

- *Hidden Brain.* A podcast exploring human behavior,
  decision-making, and the psychological factors that
  drive interactions, often relevant for profiling and
  behavioral analysis.

Documentaries and Series:

- *Inside the Criminal Mind* (Netflix). This documentary
  series explores the psychology of criminal behavior,
  profiling techniques, and case studies that highlight
  different types of offenders.

- *Mindhunter* (Netflix). Based on the work of John E.
  Douglas, this dramatized series offers insight into
  criminal profiling within the FBI, focusing on the early
  days of criminal psychology.

Online Communities and Forums:

- *Academy of Behavioral Profiling (ABP).* A professional organization dedicated to advancing the practice and ethics of criminal and behavioral profiling.

- *Reddit Communities (e.g., r/Psychology, r/TrueCrime).* Engage with discussions, case studies, and new research related to human behavior, profiling, and criminal psychology.

Recommended Focus Areas for Specialized Profiling Study

1. Criminal Profiling and Forensic Psychology:

- Explore resources focused on understanding criminal behavior, risk assessment, and case analysis.

- Read books like *Forensic Psychology: A Very Short Introduction* by David Canter.

- Join professional associations like the American Academy of Forensic Sciences.

2. Personality Profiling and Assessment:

- Deepen your understanding of personality systems such as the MBTI (Myers-Briggs Type Indicator) or the Enneagram.

- Study academic papers on personality psychology and participate in workshops on personality assessment.

3. Behavioral Economics and Decision-Making:

- *Predictably Irrational: The Hidden Forces That Shape Our Decisions* by Dan Ariely explores how cognitive biases and irrational behavior influence human decisions.

- Take courses on behavioral economics to understand how people make choices and respond to incentives.

4. Nonverbal Communication and Body Language Analysis:

- Attend workshops or training sessions on nonverbal cues, facial expressions, and situational awareness.

- Practice real-world observation skills by analyzing recorded interactions and video footage.

Afterword

In an increasingly interconnected and complex world, our ability to read, understand, and connect with others is more important than ever. The tools and techniques discussed throughout this work highlight both the power and responsibility that come with profiling. When wielded responsibly, these skills can enhance empathy, facilitate communication, and offer valuable insights that lead to growth and positive change. However, it is crucial to remain mindful of the potential pitfalls—such as biases, overgeneralization, or misuse—that can arise in this field.

Every individual carries a unique story shaped by countless experiences, and every interaction is an opportunity to learn, connect, and better understand the human experience. The art of reading people is ultimately about connecting more authentically with the world around us— an endeavor that challenges us to look beyond the surface and embrace the complexity and richness of human nature.

With gratitude,

Daniel Vernan